The Cleansing of America

a sequel to
THE MAJESTY OF GOD'S LAW

by

W. CLEON SKOUSEN

Valor Publishing Group, LLC

The Cleansing of America

Published by Valor Publishing Group, LLC
P.O. Box 2516
Orem, Utah 84059-2516

Hardcover edition ISBN: 978-1-935546-21-4

Printed in the United States of America
Year of first printing: 2010

This book is dedicated to our 50 grandchildren
and 110 great-grandchildren,
who may live to see many of these
prophecies come to pass.

PREFACE TO THE FIRST EDITION

The Cleansing of America is the culmination of several years of research, writing, and speaking on the subject of prophecy and the latter days relative to the United States, by W. Cleon Skousen. In 1994, he compiled his research as a book that he published privately for his family. He told them he didn't feel comfortable going public with it until "the time was right."

When the family asked when that "right time" would be, he said, "You will know. It will be a dark time when the Constitution is being abandoned, when economic turmoil boils on every level of society and government. It will be a time when people give up hope. The nation will be in the grip of a dark collapse. The people will begin to panic and wonder and start making foolish mistakes. They will abandon correct principles for patchwork solutions that only make things worse. You'll know it when you see it. That's the time that this book should be published."

With those predicted events now beginning to unfold in the United States and elsewhere around the world, Dr. Skousen's family members believe the time is right to publish this book. It is offered with the hope that it might edify, give encouragement, and provide direction to those wondering about prophecies of the latter days and the cleansing of America.

As with all of Dr. Skousen's previous books, this volume would have undergone his final refining touches had he lived to make them. However, editing changes were implemented after his passing, and every effort was made to preserve the author's voice and intent. As such, it is presented as he left it on January 9, 2006, the day of his passing, and just eleven days shy of his 93rd birthday.

CONTENTS

CHAPTER THREE:
The Amazing Tenth Article of Faith

CHAPTER FOUR:
Seven Steps in Setting Up God's Law

CHAPTER FIVE:
A Duel Economic System Under God's Law 85

CHAPTER SIX:
The Law of Consecration 101

INTRODUCTION

This book is a sequel to *The Majesty of God's Law*.

In reality, it is what Paul Harvey calls, "The rest of the story." In *The Majesty of God's Law*, we relied almost entirely on the Bible and standard secular sources. However, when it comes to the latest information available concerning the prophetic future of America, we had to turn to the marvelous resources which have come as a result of the Restoration.

It was Peter who talked about the "restitution of all things," [1] and what he had in mind has now been going on for more than 165 years. As a result, we have received a whole treasure of new knowledge, and this provides us with many details concerning our own day which were not available in the Bible. Many of these details will be found in this book with sources cited.

It should also be mentioned that the seven chapters in this book are seven independent lectures addressing a common subject from different perspectives. The central theme is the preparation of this land for six major purposes:

1. The restoration of the Constitution.

2. The adoption of God's law.

3. The introduction of a Zion society under the law of consecration with individual stewardships.

4. The great last gathering of Israel.

5. The coming of the ten tribes.

6. The building of the New Jerusalem.

Because these chapters focus on a common theme, it was necessary to repeat some of the sources and also use a few of the topical discussions referred to in other lectures in order to attain clarity and comprehension of the subject matter as the presentation unfolds.

At the close of each chapter, I have included a variety of questions to emphasize specific themes and suggest various topics for group discussions.

I am very grateful to my wife and several members of my family for their wonderful assistance and support in bringing this study to its final conclusion.

W. Cleon Skousen

August 13, 1994

NOTE: Throughout this book, Dr. Skousen's repeated reference to the Church refers to The Church of Jesus Christ of Latter-day Saints, unless otherwise specified.

---

1.   Acts 3:21

CHAPTER ONE

WHAT ABOUT THE FUTURE OF AMERICA?

Based on the writings of the prophets, the divine destiny of America cannot be completely realized until at least nine things have happened. Let us list the events and then we will see what the Lord and His prophets have said about them.

FIRST: The message of the restored gospel must FLOOD THE EARTH in order to search out the remnants of Israel and prepare them for the great last gathering. Since 1989, nearly the whole world has been gradually opening up so this could be accomplished.

SECOND: The great gathering cannot take place until America has been cleansed. This refers to the near future when the "time of the Gentiles" in America will be "fulfilled." At that time the wickedness of the Gentiles will have so thoroughly "sinned against the gospel" and "desecrated the land" that it will go beyond the further endurance of God.

THIRD: The Lord says the means by which America will be cleansed includes a desolating scourge which will eliminate the elements of wickedness among the Gentiles as well as the members of the Church.

FOURTH: Once America is cleansed, the worldwide call will then go out to the members of the Church to flee to America before it is too late. This call will also invite all those who do not want to be drafted into the military world dictatorship to flee to America before it is sealed off.

FIFTH: The western hemisphere will then be sealed off so that it cannot be attacked because of the "roaring seas" which will prevent anyone from reaching America either by sea or by air.

SIXTH: The scripture says at that time America then will be the only place on the face of the earth where there will be peace. This will allow the people to be organized according to God's law. Zion cities will be built up to provide freedom, peace, and prosperity for the inhabitants of all faiths, and a New Jerusalem will be set up as the capital to govern the entire land.

SEVENTH: After the Battle of Armageddon, Jesus will appear to the Jews, and the leaders of the military dictatorship will be wiped out. With only a sixth of the army surviving, the battered remnants will flee back to their homes. America will no longer need to be sealed off, and thereafter the New Jerusalem in America will be the ZION from which "shall go forth the law" with "the word of the Lord from Jerusalem." [1]

EIGHTH: After the fall of Gog and Magog following the Battle of Armageddon, the remnants of the remaining nations will be fighting and quarreling amongst themselves. Meanwhile, the ten tribes will make their miraculous journey to the temples in America. Twelve thousand will be chosen from each of the tribes and these 144,000 will go out among the nations to warn them for the last time. Those who reject their message will be sealed up to destruction at the time of Christ's Second Coming.

NINTH: Just before the Second Coming, there will be many gigantic changes on the surface of the earth. The continents and islands will become one land, the mountains will be lowered, the seas will be forced back to the poles, and the earth will be restored to its paradisiacal glory, just as it was before the Fall. The Lord says all of this must occur before the ushering in of the Millennium.

Keeping each of these prophesied events in mind, let us see where we are now on the Lord's prophetic time table and what the scriptures say we can expect in the future.

THE SIGNS OF THE TIMES

The hedonistic disintegration of the American culture during recent years is virtually unbelievable. All the elements of rot and corruption, which have destroyed three previous civilizations on this continent, are now spreading the same poisonous decadence on every level of American society.

Who would ever have guessed that America would outlaw prayer, Bible reading, or the display of the Ten Commandments in public schools? Or legalize the abortion of forty million American babies in a single generation? Or tolerate a flood of murders, robberies, violent assaults, and rapes exceeding that of any other nation in the world? Or who would have thought that with the hundreds of millions spent to build prisons, the most dangerous types of criminals would be turned loose on the streets because officials claimed they had no room to hold them? Or who would have believed the filth pouring forth from books, magazines, television, and motion pictures? Or the thousands of children being sexually abused, even by their own parents? Or the legalizing of sodomy as an optional judicially protected lifestyle and calling it part of the "new morality"?

Decent people are desperately wondering how long can this continue? What will it take to turn around such things?

God knows what it will take to turn America back from the brink of destruction toward which the nation is presently plunging. And there is not a single prophet who saw a vision of our times who did not leave a blazing warning of the consequences if we do not ask

God to forgive us, then turn back. Of course, all of the prophets said the volcanic avalanche of divine judgment could be averted by universal repentance. Tragically, however, not one of these prophets left a glimmer of hope that this people, as a nation, would do it. Nevertheless, that possibility is out there.

AN ANCIENT PROPHET IS SHOWN THE WICKEDNESS OF MODERN AMERICAN GENTILES

The last prophet of the Nephites was Moroni. He was shown a vision of the wickedness of the modern American Gentiles—and we recall that "Gentiles" are defined as those who are "strangers" to God's law and its pattern of righteous living. [2] Moroni wrote:

"Behold, Jesus Christ hath shown you unto me, and I know your doing. And I know that ye do walk in the pride of your hearts; and there are none save a few only who do not lift themselves up in the pride of their hearts, unto the wearing of fine apparel, unto envying and strifes, and malice, and iniquities." [3]

Moroni saw murderous secret combinations set up by the Gentiles in America and elsewhere. He wrote:

"O ye Gentiles, it is wisdom in God that these things should be shown unto you, that thereby ye may repent of your sins, and suffer not that these murderous combinations shall get above you, which are built up to get power and gain . . . and the work, yea, even the work of destruction come upon you, yea, even the sword of the justice of the Eternal God shall fall upon you, TO YOUR OVERTHROW AND DESTRUCTION if ye shall suffer these things to be.

"Wherefore, the Lord commandeth you, when ye shall see these things come among you that ye shall awake to a sense of your awful situation, because of this secret combination which shall be among you; or WO BE UNTO IT. . . .

"For it cometh to pass that whoso buildeth it up seeketh to overthrow the freedom of all lands, nations, and countries; and it bringeth to pass the destruction of all people, for it is built up by the devil, who is the father of all lies; even that same liar who beguiled our first parents, yea, even that same liar who hath caused man to commit murder from the beginning." [4]

GOD'S WARNING TO THE AMERICAN GENTILES

Nephi was shown that America would be discovered by the Gentiles and they would become a mighty people upon this land. [5] However, the Lord also told His prophets that the Gentiles would not have a permanent inheritance in America unless they obeyed God's commandments and accepted the gospel which would be restored in America during the latter days. [6]

In fact, the eye of prophecy pointed to a time when the Gentiles would treat the ideals of the gospel with utter contempt and thereby lose their inheritance in America. Jesus Christ foresaw the very things which are happening today and said:

"At that day when the Gentiles shall sin against my gospel, and shall reject the fullness of my gospel, and shall be lifted up in the pride of their hearts above all nations, and above all the people of the whole earth, and shall be filled with all manner of lyings, and of deceits, and of mischiefs, and all manner of hypocrisy, and murders, and priestcrafts, and whoredoms, and of secret abominations; and if they shall do all those things, and shall reject the fullness of my gospel, behold, saith the Father, I will bring the fullness of my gospel from among them." [7]

This last phrase, "I will bring the fullness of my gospel from among them," has always meant removing God's people and especially the missionaries from among them. Once God has gathered out His people from the midst of the wicked, God's cleansing will be imminent.

Notice in the scripture we have just quoted that it says, the "Gentiles shall sin against my gospel." We cannot help wondering what that might mean.

Massive Attacks Against God's Law in the Twentieth Century

In the early days of this nation, the Bible-reading, Christian-oriented people prevailed in nearly every segment of the nation. Gradually, however, the evils of a hostile Gentile culture began to hover over the nation like an ominous cloud. As we move into the early years of the twenty-first century, we find Gentile wickedness, violence, and crime penetrating the fabric of nearly every dimension of our national culture.

This came about as a result of a carefully contrived attack on the very foundation of America as perceived by the Founding Fathers. These evil Gentile master planners aimed their attack at God's standard of morality, God's value of human life, and God's code of divine law. In fact these people—whom the scriptures refer to as "gentiles"—boldly ridiculed the idea of there even being a God. This anti-theistic propaganda spread into the colleges and universities, and even took root in some of the major churches. After two generations, the famous philosopher, Friedrich Nietzsche, felt their campaign had been so successful that he arrogantly announced, "God is dead!" Then he went insane. [8]

Atheism has remained the very foundation of the gentile culture and the latest trend is to glamorize its philosophy under the title of "Secular Humanism." But there is no attempt to hide its fundamental beliefs. [9] In its two official "manifestos" it projects the following:

1. There is no God.

2. Man has no soul and therefore no immortality.

3. Man must be his own savior.

4. No act is sin in and of itself.

5. Prayer is ineffectual.

6. There were never any miracles.

7. There was never a divine creation.

8. There is no "last judgment."

9. The Bible is merely a composition of man-made writings.

10. The morals of the Bible are puritanical and outdated.

As we previously indicated, some of the major religious denominations have gradually surrendered many of their biblical beliefs to Secular Humanism. This was reflected in a poll of the delegates at a convention of the National Council of Churches, indicating: [10]

33% denied the existence of God.

36% expressed doubt about the deity of Christ.

31% doubted life after death.

62% questioned the miracles.

77% denied the existence of a devil.

Of course, we scarcely need to be reminded that atheism constituted the cornerstone of Marx's International Communism in the Soviet Union and China; Hitler's Nazism in Germany; and Mussolini's Fascism in Italy. It also dominated the thinking in many of the democratic socialist countries of Europe. Eventually these politically powerful atheistic forces combined to take over more than a third of the entire human race.

SIGMUND FREUD

Meanwhile, the intellectual world embellished its anti-theistic thinking with the books of two famous men who totally devastated the Judeo-Christian beliefs of millions of people. The first of these two men was Sigmund Freud (1856-1939). He graduated from medical school in Vienna, Austria, and developed a revolutionary approach to the normal pressures of life by applying certain principles which he called "psychoanalysis."

His theories were based on the premise that individual mental health requires that a person must accommodate or ameliorate the frustrating impulses which prey upon us, the most powerful of which is the sex drive. Freud called a person's sex drive the "libido." According to Freud, the idea of uninhibited sex or total sexual gratification is a "scientific" requirement for sound mental health.

In fact, researchers have found that Freud was deeply concerned about his own "libido." For fifteen years he was a heavy user of cocaine, thinking it would increase his sexual drive.

Of course, Freud's theories and practices played havoc with the Ten Commandments and Christian restraints designed to curb urges which violate God's law.

But it was not until after Freud had died in 1939 that his theories came under the close scrutiny of many professional analysts. When Dr. E. Fuller Torrey came out with his report on what he discovered from a study of Freud, he was so angry he called his book *Freudian Fraud—The Malignant Effect of Freud's Theory on American Thought and Culture.* [11]

ALFRED C. KINSEY

Meanwhile, another alleged "scientist" picked up where Freud left off and created a cultural shock even greater than Freud. His name was Alfred C. Kinsey, and he was originally associated with the University of Indiana as a professor of zoology but eventually induced the university to finance him as head of an Institute for Sexual Research. He and his associates then claimed they were conducting—for the first time in history—a study of human sexual behavior.

He published The Sexual Behavior of the Human Male in 1948 and The Sexual Behavior of the Human Female in 1953. Both books were later combined into what became known as "The Kinsey Report."

What shocked America were his alleged statistics, which proved "scientifically" that homosexuality, promiscuity, and pedophilia (sex with children) were much more widespread than anyone had suspected. It later turned out that many of his interviews were with prison inmates, prostitutes, and other subjects who were far from representative of the general population.

When Dr. Judith A. Reisman and three associates investigated Kinsey's Institute and discovered the reckless and incompetent manner in which he had put together his so-called "scientific" statistics, they published a book called, Kinsey, Sex and Fraud—the Indoctrination of a People. [12]

The "people," of course, were primarily the Americans who had fallen for Kinsey as an alleged expert. After all, he had published pages of statistics to prove that "everybody is doing it, so why are you missing out?" And that is exactly the way his book was interpreted by the public. It was a best-seller overnight.

Little did the people realize all the principles and practices Kinsey was trying to inject into the American culture. It turned out that he wanted people to look at themselves as "animals" who had natural proclivities with tensions and urges that needed to be released by whatever means necessary.

All of the hedonistic practices which are labeled in the Bible as an "abomination unto God" were portrayed by Kinsey and his associates as not only normal and pleasurable, but widely practiced.

Dr. Reisman and her associates found that Kinsey's Institute had observed or been present when criminal sexual abuse was perpetrated on numerous children or pre-adolescent youth in an effort to prove that children are born with the capability of becoming fully active sexually. [13] The idea was to encourage their participation in sexual stimulation at an early age. Like Freud, Kinsey recommended sex education to promote and excite sexual interest among children.

Members of the Kinsey entourage even went further. They felt parents or other adults should take children in hand and participate with them in sexual relations at an early age so their sexual development would mature "normally and naturally." Their goal was to have universal sex education in the schools so the next generation would accept whatever sexual lifestyle a person might choose as entirely legitimate.

POPULARIZING ABJECT IMMORALITY

Between Freud and Kinsey, a complete revolution occurred in the minds of the upcoming generation concerning sexual indulgence. Traditional Christian elements in America strongly protested, but Freud's "scientific" justification, labeling promiscuity a necessity, combined with Kinsey's rigged statistics indicating that "everybody's doing it," overwhelmed the opposition as being "prudish" and "old-fashioned."

Dr. Reisman gives the following appraisal of the Freud and Kinsey legacy:

"Socially, the sexual revolution has wrought upheaval. There are about 11 to 12 million sexually active adolescents in the U.S . . . About 860,000 teenagers will become pregnant this year— 23,000 aged 14 or younger. More than 40% of pregnancies in 15 to 19-year-olds will be aborted and 60% of those in girls under 15. . . .

"Between 1950 and 1968 the number of out-of-wedlock births to teenagers almost tripled to about 165,000 per year . . . Today there will be about 230,000 births per year to women under 20 who are both poor and unmarried, a testimony to the significantly increased rates of sexual activity among teenage females." [14]

In this same text, we find numerous reports containing overwhelming evidence of depravity and social disintegration all across the cultural spectrum. Official statistics show:

Criminal sexual assaults on women increased 526% between

1960 and 1986.

Centers for Disease Control reported 2.5 million teenagers who had sexually transmitted diseases in 1987 (excluding AIDS/HIV).

AIDS, an incurable disease, has now spread among so many voters that in some areas candidates cannot be elected without their support. The political power of the gay constituency has become so powerful that AIDS is the only highly contagious disease that has escaped quarantine regulations.

Hepatitis B has become an epidemic among the homosexual population. Transmission is by blood, semen, or saliva. There are about 200,000 new infections annually in the U.S.

Adolescent suicides have increased 300%. In the last thirty years, crimes of violence—such as murder, robbery, rape, etc.—have increased 500%. [15]

THE UGLY IMAGE OF A GENTILE CULTURE

The social disintegration that has taken place in America during the last half of the twentieth century is characteristic of twenty-two earlier civilizations that are now extinct.

The prophets of the past who saw our day in vision warned that if a hostile Gentile culture erupted in America, it would not be endured for long. Think of this generation already aborting more than 40 million babies. This culture of depravity is being perpetuated by leaders and teachers who are corrupting millions of youth.

It is clear that we are approaching the time when God's cup of wrath and indignation might overflow at any time, just as the prophets predicted.

HOW WILL AMERICA BE CLEANSED?

The prophets not only predicted that there would be a thorough cleansing of America, but they described how it would occur. The Lord's cleansing will include the destabilizing impact of earthquakes, tornadoes, famine, riots, and civil strife. But the primary destruction will come from a massive, cataclysmic plague. The Lord refers to it as an "overflowing" or "desolating scourge." [16] The Bubonic Plague wiped out nearly half of Europe in a very short time, but the plague predicted for the cleansing of America sounds far worse.

Here is the way the Lord speaks of it:

"And when the times of the Gentiles is come in, a light shall break forth among them that sit in darkness, and it shall be the fulness of my gospel; But they receive it not; for they perceive not the light, and they turn their hearts from me because of the precepts of men.

"And in that generation shall the times of the Gentiles be fulfilled. And there shall be men standing in that generation, that shall not pass til they shall see an OVERFLOWING SCOURGE; for a desolating sickness shall cover the land." [17]

This overflowing scourge is intended to cleanse and scour America of its wickedness. Therefore, the Lord said to the members of the restored Church in modern times:

"Bring forth fruit meet for their Father's kingdom; otherwise there remaineth a SCOURGE and judgment to be poured out upon the children of Zion." [18]

And finally:

"All the wicked shall mourn. For behold, and lo, vengeance cometh speedily upon the ungodly as the whirlwind; and who shall escape it?

"The Lord's SCOURGE shall pass over by night and by day, and the report thereof shall vex all people." [19]

THE CHURCH IS CLEANSED OF APOSTATES
AND BACKSLIDERS

The Lord also warned that the cleansing would not begin among the Gentiles but it would commence among the wicked of His own church and then spread to the wicked throughout the land. [20] Consider the following:

"Behold, vengeance cometh speedily upon the inhabitants of the earth . . . And upon MY HOUSE shall it begin, and from MY HOUSE shall it go forth, saith the Lord; First among those among you, saith the Lord, who have professed to know my name and have not known me, and have blasphemed against me in the midst of my house, saith the Lord." [21]

A person blasphemes against the Lord in the midst of His house (the temple) when he or she is unworthy but gains admission to the temple by lying to the bishop and stake president. A person also blasphemes the name of the Lord when he or she makes sacred covenants in the temple and then profanes them.

That the Lord's judgment should begin with the cleansing of His own temple before the plague spreads to the rest of the country was known to the Apostle Peter. He said:

"For the time is come that judgment must begin at the house of God: and if it first begin at us, what shall the end be of them that obey not the gospel of God? And if the righteous scarcely be saved, where shall the ungodly and the sinner appear?" [22]

In the following vision, we learn how the terrible scourge spoken of in the scriptures actually commences in the region of the Lord's house in America and then sweeps out among the wicked from coast to coast and from pole to pole.

THE VISION OF JOHN TAYLOR

On December 16, 1877, a leader of the Church saw a night vision which Wilford Woodruff copied into his Journal on June

15, 1878. This vision is attributed to John Taylor, who was then President of the Quorum of the Twelve and was later ordained President of the Church in October, 1880. Here are the circumstances which have led to the conclusion that this vision was received by John Taylor:

The person who received this vision said he had been studying the "Revelations in French." John Taylor, although not named by Wilford Woodruff, was the one apostle who was familiar with the French language. He opened the French mission in 1850 and served as its president until 1852. During that time he published a French missionary magazine, and published a French translation of the Book of Mormon. From this background, it will be understood why this writer agrees with others in referring to the following vision as "the John Taylor Vision."

The record of this vision is as follows:

"I had been reading the Revelations in the French language. My mind was calm more so than usual . . . It seemed as though I was lifted out of myself . . . I was immediately in Salt Lake City wandering about the streets . . . On the door of every house I found a badge of mourning . . . I then looked in all directions over the Territory, East, West, North and South, and I found the same mourning in every place throughout the land . . . It seemed as though I was above the earth, looking down to it as I passed along on my way east and I saw the roads full of people principally women with just what they could carry in bundles on their backs travelling to the mountains on foot . . . It did not seem as though the [railroad] cars were running. The rails looked rusty, and the road abandoned. . . .

"The next [place] I saw was Washington, and I found the city a desolation—the White House empty. The halls of Congress the same. Everything in ruins. The people seemed to have fled the city and left it to take care of itself.

"I was next in the city of Baltimore and in the square where the monument of [the War of] 1812 stands, in front of St. Charles and other hotels, I saw the dead piled up so high as to fill the square . . . The waters of the Chesapeake [Bay] and of the city were so stagnant and such a stench arose from them on account of the putrefying of dead bodies that the very smell caused death. . . . Again I saw no men except they were dead, lying in the streets, and very few women . . . It was horrible, beyond description to look at.

"In Philadelphia . . . everything was still. No living soul was to be seen to greet me, and it seemed as though the whole city was without an inhabitant . . . Everywhere I went the putrefying of the dead bodies caused such a stench that it was impossible for any creature to exist alive, nor did I see any living thing in the city."

Following this, he was shown New York City in total ruin. He continues:

"I was given to understand, that the same horror was being enacted all over the country, North, South, East and West, that few were left alive. Still there were some." [23]

One of the most important segments of this vision came next:

"Immediately after I seemed to be standing on the west bank of the Missouri River opposite the city of Independence, but I saw no city. I saw the whole states of Missouri and Illinois and part of Iowa were a complete wilderness with no living human being in them.

"I then saw a short distance from the river twelve men dressed in the robes of the temple standing in a square or nearly so. I understood it represented the twelve gates of the New Jerusalem, and they were with hands uplifted consecrating the ground and laying the cornerstones. I saw myriads of angels hovering over them and around about them and also an immense pillar of a cloud over them and I heard the singing of the most beautiful music the words, 'Now is established the Kingdom of our God and his Christ and he shall reign forever and ever, and the kingdom shall never be thrown down for the Saints have overcome.'

"I saw people coming from the river and different places a long way off to help build the temple, and it seemed that the hosts of the angels also helped to get the material to build the temple." [24]

As the vision came to a close, President Taylor found himself back in Utah.

Wilford Woodruff may have been especially attracted to this vision and took the time carefully to copy it into his journal because he, himself, was already well aware of how America would be cleansed and how terrible it would be. In fact, in 1832, the Lord had referred to three of the great cities in the East that would be destroyed—namely New York, Albany, and Boston. He told his servants to warn these cities "of the desolation and utter abolishment which await them" if they rejected God's latter-day message. [25] We know from Wilford Woodruff's own writings and speeches that he had seen much of what John Taylor saw.

For example, on August 22, 1863, Wilford Woodruff prophesied about people in the future who would be talking about the period in which we are now living, and say:

"It was before Boston was swept into the sea, and the sea heaving itself beyond its bounds; it was before Albany was destroyed by fire." [26]

As for New York—which was also mentioned by the Lord— Orson Pratt prophesied:

"The great, powerful and populous city of New York . . . will in a few years become a mass of ruins. The people will wonder while gazing on the ruins that cost hundreds of millions to build, what has become of its inhabitants." [27]

THE VISION OF PATRIARCH CHARLES D. EVANS

A vision similar to that of John Taylor—but with additional details—is reported to have been given to Patriarch Charles D. Evans of Springville, Utah. It was published in the unofficial LDS magazine, The Contributor, of August, 1894. [28] Patriarch Evans describes how the plague decimated its victims. He said the malady began with:

"A purple spot which appeared on the cheek, or on the back of the hand, and which invariably enlarged until it spread over the entire surface of the body, producing certain death . . . This plague in grown persons rotted the eyes in the sockets and consumed the tongue as would a powerful acid." [29]

He said, "Other plagues followed I forbear to record." [30]

Patriarch Evans observed that in due time, the plague began to abate in the mountain region where it first began, and the survivors commenced to get everything back in order. In fact, he concludes his report of the vision on an encouraging note. He saw that when peace was finally established, the beautiful New Jerusalem was built up and Zion cities rapidly spread out across the land.

He was deeply impressed by the fact that the schools used "urims" to teach events of the past and provide the students with penetrating insights into physical matter which greatly facilitated the study of chemistry, physiology, and medicine. [31] But let us go back to see what the Lord said concerning the cleansing process that would precede these more pleasant events.

THE WORD OF THE LORD CONCERNING THE CLEANSING OF AMERICA

Important revelations which correspond with the two visions we have just discussed provide explicit details of what can be expected during the cleansing process. One revelation says:

"And there shall be weeping and wailing among the hosts of men; And there shall be a great hailstorm sent forth to destroy the crops of the earth . . . Wherefore, I the Lord God will send forth flies upon the face of the earth, which shall take hold of the inhabitants thereof, and shall eat their flesh, and shall cause maggots to come in upon them;

"And their tongues shall be stayed that they shall not utter against me; and their flesh shall fall from off their bones, and their eyes from their sockets." [32]

On another occasion, the Lord said:

"And in that generation shall the times of the Gentiles be fulfilled. And there shall be men standing in that generation, that shall not pass until they shall see an overflowing scourge; for a desolating sickness shall cover the land. But my disciples shall stand in holy places, and shall not be moved; but among the wicked, men shall lift up their voices and curse God and die. And there shall be earthquakes also in divers places, and many desolations. . . ." [33]

JOSEPH SMITH KNEW THERE WOULD BE TWO GREAT CRISES IN AMERICAN HISTORY

On December 25, 1832, Joseph Smith was told about a terrible civil war that eventually would threaten to destroy the United States. He was told where it would start, how the country would be divided, and that, eventually, it would result in "the death and misery of many souls." [34]

In this same revelation, there is a prediction of coming world wars, [35] and then a reference to a series of catastrophic events and the affliction of warfare that will eventually "make an end of all nations." [36]

Joseph Smith knew many details concerning this second crisis insofar as the United States would be concerned. On January 4, 1833, just ten days after the Revelation on War referred to above, Joseph Smith wrote:

"And now I am prepared to say by the authority of Jesus Christ, that not many years shall pass away before the United States shall present such a scene of bloodshed as has not a parallel in the history of our nation; pestilence, hail, famine, and earthquake will sweep the wicked of this generation from off the face of the land, to open and prepare the way for the return of the lost tribes of Israel from the north country . . . Repent ye, repent ye, and embrace the everlasting covenant, and FLEE TO ZION BEFORE THE OVERFLOWING SCOURGE OVERTAKES YOU." [37]

Notice that in the Civil War, the military conflict took upwards of 600,000 lives, but the nation survived. In the subsequent crisis incidental to the cleansing of America, Joseph Smith speaks of an "overflowing scourge" that will depopulate much of the nation and be accompanied by "pestilence, hail, famine, and earthquake." This ominous prophecy remains to be fulfilled sometime in the future.

At this point in our narration, we cannot help but ask, "Then what happens?" At last we get the good news.

* * * *

TOPICS FOR REFLECTION AND DISCUSSION

1. Can you itemize in order the nine events which the prophets said would occur prior to the Second Coming?

2. What specific "signs of the times" would you consider to be reprehensible to God? Did the ancient prophets know that the American nation would become wicked?

3. How extensive was the impact of the philosophy of atheism in America? How much of the earth did the political advocates of atheism occupy? What did Friedrich Nietzsche mean when he said "God is dead?" What are some of the major beliefs of the Secular Humanists? To what extent have some of the major denominations picked up these ideas?

4. Describe the background of Sigmund Freud and describe why his ideas had such a denigrating impact on millions of people.

5. What was there about the Kinsey Report that so seriously destabilized the American culture? Why would millions of people change their lifestyle just because Kinsey claimed "everybody's doing it?"

6. How does the Lord define a "Gentile?" Was America discovered and developed by righteous "Gentiles"? Did God warn them that they might lose their inheritance in America?

7. How did the Lord say America would be cleansed? Describe what impressed you most about the vision of John Taylor. List three highlights in the vision of Patriarch Charles D. Evans.

8. Why does the Lord say the cleansing of America will commence with His own people?

9. What were the two great historical events which Joseph Smith knew would happen to America? Which one is still in the future?

10. What do you feel you should be doing to prepare for the cleansing of America? What should you be doing to help the Church prepare for the cleansing of America?

---

1.   Isaiah 2:3

2.   See *strangers* as discussed in Lev. 22, Deut. 24, Exodus 12

3.   Mormon 8:35-36, emphasis added

4.   Ether 8:23–25

5.   1 Nephi 13:12-19

6.   2 Nephi 1:5

7.   3 Nephi 16:10

8.   Skousen, *The Naked Communist*, Salt Lake City: The Ensign Publishing Company, 1962, pp.350-352

9.   Abstracted from the official statements found in *Humanist Manifesto I* and *Humanist Manifesto II*

10. Homer Duncan, Lubbock, Texas, *Secular Humanism, The Missionary Crusader*, 1979, p. 36

11. New York: Harper-Collins Publishers, 1992

12. Dr. Judith A. Reisman, Edward W. Eichel, Dr. John H. Court & Dr. J. Gordon Muir, Lafayette, La.:Lochinvar-Huntington House Publications, 1990

13. Ibid. pp.. 8, 29-31

14. Ibid. p. 87

15. According to the Centers for Disease Control (CDC), sexual activity among teens continues to be a serious problem in the U.S. For example, in 2007, almost 48% of all adolescents age 15-19 were sexually active, 15% of those with 4 or more partners. In 2005, about 400,000 unmarried teens had abortions. Since 2000, an average of 8 million in the 15-24 age group become infected with a sexually transmitted disease (STD) each year. Since 2001, suicide has been the third highest cause of death among teens. See www.cdc.gov and www.census.gov for more information.

16. D&C 45:31; 84:58; Isaiah 28:18

17. D&C 45:28–31

18. D&C 84:58

19. D&C 97:21–23

20. D&C 112:25

21. D&C 112:24–26

22. 1 Peter 4:17-18

23. *Wilford Woodruff Journal*, Scott G. Kenney, ed., Midvale, Utah, Signature Books,1985, vol. 7, pp. 419-423. The spelling has been corrected.

24. Ibid.

25. D&C 84:114

26. *Journal of Discourses*, vol. 21:299

27. *Journal of Discourses*, vol. 12:344

28. *The Contributor*, vol. 15, pp. 638-641; this unofficial LDS publication was a precursor to *The Improvement Era*

29. Ibid.

30. Ibid.

31. Ibid. See the full account of Patriarch Evans' dream in the Appendix

32. D&C 29:15–19

33. D&C 45:30–33

34. D&C 87:1

35. Ibid. v.3

36. Ibid. v.7

37. 1938. Teachings of the Prophet Joseph Smith, Section One 1830-1834. Doctrinal History of the Church, 1:315, emphasis added. Deseret Book Company, Salt Lake City

CHAPTER TWO

AMERICA BEGINS TO ATTAIN HER MANIFEST DESTINY

As soon as America is cleansed sufficiently, God will commence the next important stage of what Isaiah called "a marvelous work and a wonder." [1] Two things will happen in quick succession.

First, the Lord will bring a great multitude of new inhabitants to America to join with those who survived the cleansing.

Second, He then will seal off the western hemisphere so it cannot be attacked while the Lord is setting up the foundation for a glorious civilization to be known as Zion. In the midst of it, He will have His servants build a great metropolis to be known as the New Jerusalem.

A FLOOD OF NEW INHABITANTS WILL COME TO AMERICA

The scriptures tell us that as soon as America has been cleansed of the Gentile wickedness which contaminated her, the Lord will undertake to bring all the members of His Church from Europe, Asia, and the islands of the sea to "the land . . . choice above all other lands." [2]

The Lord will also invite all the peace-loving non-members of the Church to flee to America. Otherwise Gog—which means the prince of the Gentiles—will conscript them into his monstrous military "abomination of desolation." [3] John said this vast army would ultimately comprise 200,000,000 men under arms. [4]

In a modern revelation, the Lord refers to this time when all of these millions will be gathered out of the world to flee to America. He said:

"And it shall come to pass among the wicked, that every man that will not take his sword against his neighbor must needs flee unto Zion for safety. And there shall be gathered unto it out of every nation under heaven; and it shall be the only people that shall not be at war one with another." [5]

Another scripture indicates that this gathering "out of every nation under heaven" will include the members of the Church. When the Lord showed Enoch a vision of our day, he was allowed to see that in the latter days the Church would flood the earth with the message of the restored gospel, and then the Lord explained what would follow. He told Enoch that His purpose in flooding the earth with the gospel in the latter days was to:

". . . gather out mine elect [the converts to the gospel] from the four quarters of the earth, unto a place which I shall prepare, a Holy City, that my people may gird up their loins, and be looking forth for the time of my coming; for there shall be my tabernacle, and it shall be called Zion, a New Jerusalem." [6]

Joseph Smith added this interesting detail concerning the time of the gathering:

"The last revelation says, Ye shall not have time to have gone over the earth until these things [the great gathering] come." [7]

This would indicate that the missionaries barely will be getting into the last nations when the call goes out, "Gather to Zion." All of this pertains to our day, since we are now flooding the earth with the gospel. It is highly significant that just about the time we are reaching the last few nations, the Saints in Europe, Asia, and the islands of the sea will be instructed to flee to America before it is too late.

SEALING OFF THE WESTERN HEMISPHERE

The urgency which will compel the multitudes to hasten their flight to America will be the Lord's warning that the waters surrounding the western hemisphere will soon become so violent that no one will be able to reach Zion by air or by sea.

Luke speaks of these latter days when:

"There shall be signs . . . [in the heavens] and upon the earth distress of nations, with perplexity; THE SEA AND THE WAVES ROARING." [8]

In a modern revelation, the Lord refers to this critical time:

"Wherefore, the days will come that no flesh shall be safe upon the waters. And it shall be said in days to come that none is able to go up to the land of Zion upon the waters, but he that is upright in heart." [9]

The emphasis here is on the danger of travel by water, but since these storms are so violent that Zion is sealed off, it would imply that the isolation would apply to air as well.

Another scripture implying complete isolation of the western hemisphere is the Lord's statement we have already quoted which says:

"And there shall be gathered unto it out of every nation under heaven; and it shall be the ONLY people that shall not be at war one with another." [10]

This means that those who have responded to the Lord's call and hastened to America will have the peaceful security of being sealed off from the rest of the world so they can lay the foundation for a whole new civilization.

Early Gathering To The Mountain West

As these multitudes migrate to America, their inclination will be to gather in the mountain west. Isaiah saw it happening and said:

"He that walketh righteously . . . shall dwell on high: his place of defence shall be the munitions of rocks: bread shall be given him; his waters shall be sure." [11]

And in another place he says:

"And it shall come to pass in the last days, that the mountain of the LORD's house shall be established in the top of the mountains, and shall be exalted above the hills; and all nations shall flow unto it. And many people shall go and say, Come ye, and let us go up to the mountain of the LORD, to the house of the God of Jacob; and he will teach us of his ways, and we will walk in his paths." [12]

The Miracle Of The Water In The Wilderness

In our own day, one might wonder how the mountain west could accommodate the gathering of all these multitudes. For hundreds—if not for thousands—of years the mountain west has been a virtual wilderness of desert and sagebrush. But Isaiah saw it all changed. He said in the days when the gathering takes place:

". . . the desert shall blossom . . . Israel shall be gathered, and Zion shall be built up. The wilderness and the solitary place shall be glad for them; and the desert shall rejoice, and blossom as the rose. It shall blossom abundantly, and rejoice even with joy and singing." [13]

All this is made possible by the miracle of water. Isaiah describes this marvelous phenomenon, and those of us who have lived and worked on the desert appreciate what a tremendous miracle this will be. Isaiah says:

"For in the wilderness shall waters break out, and streams in the desert. And the parched ground shall become a pool, and the thirsty land springs of water: in the habitation of dragons, where each lay, shall be grass with reeds and rushes." [14]

This miracle of the water seeping up through the barren ground in the wilderness of the West will permit millions of acres to be inhabited by the gathering multitudes and allow extensive rural development where former desolation prevailed.

RUINED GENTILE CITIES TO BE REHABILITATED

However, the multitudes will be so great that eventually they will "break forth on the right and on the left," and the people will find it necessary to clean up and inhabit the great Gentile cities that were destroyed during the cleansing of the land. Isaiah says:

"Enlarge the place of thy tent, and let them stretch forth the curtains of thine habitation; spare not, lengthen thy cords, and strengthen thy stakes; For thou shalt break forth on the right hand and on the left; and thy seed shall INHERIT the GENTILES, and make the DESOLATE CITIES TO BE INHABITED." [15]

This is the passage that tells us that during the cleansing of America, the Gentile cities will be left desolate and without habitation.

THE MIRACLE OF LAW, ORDER, AND PEACE

One of the most gratifying surprises for thousands of these refugees and gathering Saints will be the phenomenon of settling down into a peaceful and orderly life.

After their immediate necessities are provided, these refugees of all faiths, as well as the gathering Saints, will be invited—along with their friends and relatives—to settle in some appropriate area. At last they and their families will be safe. As Elder Boyd K. Packer said:

"Across the world, those who now come by the tens of thousands will inevitably come as a flood to where the family is safe. Here they will worship the Father in the name of Christ, by the gift of the Holy Ghost, and know that the gospel is the great plan of happiness." [16]

We shall later study in detail this settling process and how the people of all faiths will elect their captains over each group of ten families, each group of fifty families, then a hundred families, and so forth. Very early in the settling process they will be taught God's law, and then they will be invited to enter into a covenant to keep the law.

In this environment of orderly security, the administration of the law will provide a perfect system of justice under judges or captains elected by the people themselves. Here will be an ideal opportunity to practice the Lord's basic formula for peace on earth, good will toward men. [17]

THE MIRACLE OF MINIMUM POVERTY

As we have already seen, Isaiah foresaw that the refugees and gathering Saints would come to Zion with an anxiety to be taught the new law and God's new ways of setting up a free, peaceful, prosperous society. As we mentioned earlier, Isaiah said:

"And many people shall go and say, Come ye, and let us go up to the mountain of the LORD, to the house of the God of Jacob; and he will teach us of his ways, and we will walk in his paths." [18]

God's law requires that each community share one another's problems "in common." This does not mean sharing property in common, but it does mean sharing one another's needs, especially in an emergency. There will be a strong emphasis on volunteerism, much as it was in early America. If a man's barn burned down, the whole community turned out to build a new one.

The object is to support and help one another until everyone is "settled in" and there is no poverty among them. This means that even though the standard of living may be somewhat modest in the beginning, everyone will have the basic necessities. It is up to the captains of tens, fifties, and hundreds to see that no one is neglected.

With the passing of time, everyone will gradually move from tents to cabins, and from cabins to comfortable homes with gardens, vines, and fruit trees.

THE MIRACLE OF MINIMUM CRIME

The suppression of crime is almost automatic under God's law. Those with dishonest tendencies soon learn that crime does not pay. Reparation and punitive damages all go to the victim, and the enforcement of the law is based on the principle that he who hurts must be hurt unless he or she "makes satisfaction" in terms of fines or services to the injured person.

The famous King Benjamin achieved this by strict enforcement of the law as God originally gave it to Moses. He said:

"Neither have I suffered that ye should be confined in dungeons, nor that ye should make slaves one of another, nor that ye should murder, or plunder, or steal, or commit adultery; nor even have I suffered that ye should commit any manner of wickedness, and have taught you that ye should keep the commandments of the Lord, in all things which he hath commanded you. . . .

"And even I, myself, have labored with mine own hands that I might serve you, and that ye should not be laden with taxes, and that there should nothing come upon you which was grievous to be borne . . . and of all these things which I have spoken, ye yourselves are witnesses this day." [19]

Later, the great King Mosiah was able to accomplish the same thing by strict enforcement of the law. He said to his people:

"And even I myself have labored with all the power and faculties which I have possessed, to teach you the commandments of God, and to establish peace throughout the land, that there should be no wars nor contentions, no stealing, nor plundering, nor murdering, nor any manner of iniquity;

"And whosoever has committed iniquity, him have I punished according to the crime which he has committed, according to the law which has been given to us by our fathers [and that was God's law under a system of judges!]." [20]

THE MIRACLE OF PROSPERITY

We have already mentioned a number of factors which are the underlying requirements for a prosperous community. It all begins with a spirit of mutual concern.

Brigham Young was one of America's greatest pioneers, who set up 350 successful communities in his lifetime. He emphasized that a government under God's law promotes and protects the rights of all faiths so they can live harmoniously together. He said to the members of his own church:

"If the Latter-day Saints think, when the Kingdom of God [government under God's law] is established on the earth, that all the inhabitants of the earth will join the church called Latter-day Saints, they are egregiously mistaken. I presume there will be as many sects and parties then as now." [21]

The genius of God's law is that everyone is treated with respect and their rights are protected. As an epistle from the Quorum of the Twelve clearly stated in 1847:

"The Kingdom of God [government under God's law] consists in correct principles; and it mattereth not what a man's religious faith is; whether he be a Presbyterian, or a Methodist, or a Baptist, or a Latter-day Saint . . . or a Catholic or Episcopalian . . . if he will bow the knee and with his tongue confess that Jesus is the Christ, and will support good and wholesome laws for the regulation of society—we hail him as a brother. . . ." [22]

The church leaders pointed out elsewhere that the same rights would be upheld for non-Christians who will support good laws. [23]

Another element undergirding prosperity would be circulating honest money based on gold and silver as required by the Constitution. [24]

Private banks would be chartered by states under strict regulations with a ceiling on interest.

God's law contemplates a very industrious population with full employment. All who can work, must work, to enjoy the blessings of a godly society.

IMPORTANCE OF THE PRINCIPLE OF SIMPLICITY

It will no doubt come as an astonishing surprise to those who are new to the wonders of God's law to realize how much more simple life can be than when the wicked were in charge of things.

While this writer was studying law in Washington D.C., it was appalling to discover how confused and complex our whole society had been allowed to become. By way of contrast, the genius of God's law is its simplicity. It provides:

1. A sound and much more simple system of government.

2. A sound system of law and justice based on God's law.

3. A sound money system based on a medium of exchange with inherent value.

4. A sound economic system where the Golden Rule will have an appropriate part to play.

5. A sound social structure based on righteous principles.

SETTING UP THE NEW JERUSALEM

The task of setting up the New Jerusalem will be a glorious undertaking. The scripture is clear that this project will be undertaken a short time after the cleansing of the land and the gathering of the hosts of new inhabitants to America.

It is highly significant that we have known the exact location of this future capital of the world ever since it was first revealed in 1831. [25] However, the early American colonists speculated that the New Jerusalem would be in New England. They even thought the Millennium would begin from there. However, we have this interesting comment from a certain Reverend Washington who visited the mid-west in 1890. He said:

"Here, upon these plains, the problems of history are to be solved, and here, if anywhere, is to rise the city of God, the New Jerusalem, whose glories are to fill the earth." [26]

As we have indicated, the exact site for the New Jerusalem had been revealed to the Lord's prophet sixty-seven years earlier, and it was to be on the plains of the mid-west as Reverend Washington had supposed. In fact, the spot chosen by the Lord is very close to the center of the North American continent. The government surveyors have designated the center of the North American continent with a marker located approximately three miles east of Junction City, Kansas, and less than 150 miles west of the site of the New Jerusalem. [27]

In President Taylor's vision, he said that following the cleansing of America, the region where the New Jerusalem would be built was completely barren. He observed that this was not only true of Jackson County, but several of the adjacent states were also like a wilderness. [28] Brigham Young mentions the same thing, [29] and Heber C. Kimball is quoted as saying: "The western boundaries of the state of Missouri will be swept so clean of its inhabitants that, as President Young tells, when we return to that place 'There will not be left so much as a yellow dog to wag his tail.'" [30]

This is interesting because many have visualized great crowds surging back to Jackson County immediately after the cleansing to participate in the building of the New Jerusalem. All of the known circumstances suggest that to participate in this undertaking, only special individuals will be called—as they are needed—to lay the foundation for this great city.

THE CONFERENCE AT ADAM-ONDI-AHMAN

It is this writer's opinion that it will be under these circumstances that the long-awaited conference of God's leading prophets from Adam to the present will convene about this time at Adam-ondi-Ahman. During this sacred meeting, the keys of each dispensation will be returned to Adam, and he will turn them over to the Savior. From that moment on, Lucifer will begin to lose his dominion over the earth. [31] It would appear that this conference occurs before this region has been repopulated. As Joseph Fielding Smith has written:

"When this gathering is held, the world will not know of it; the members of the Church at large will not know of it . . . The Saints cannot know of it—except those who officially shall be called into this council—for it shall precede the coming of Jesus Christ as a thief in the night, unbeknown to all the world." [32]

It would seem appropriate that this great conference would occur just as the foundation for the New Jerusalem is being laid and at the very moment when the governments of the wicked are beginning to crumble to pieces. When Daniel saw a vision of the conference at Adam-ondi-Ahman, he wrote:

"I beheld till THE THRONES WERE CAST DOWN, and the Ancient of days did sit." [33]

It seems significant that the meeting at Adam-ondi-Ahman should take place just about the time when Gog and all his conquered kingdoms will be crumbling. No longer will America need to be sealed off by "roaring seas." [34]

From that time on, the New Jerusalem can gradually expand its influence until it becomes the political capital of the world. The Old Jerusalem will be the spiritual headquarters of the Savior so—as we have mentioned earlier—the words of Isaiah will be literally fulfilled when he said:

"Out of Zion shall go forth the law, and the word of the Lord from Jerusalem." [35]

THE UNIQUE FEATURES OF THE NEW JERUSALEM

As early as 1832, Joseph Smith was given the layout for a Zion city and a copy was sent to Missouri by the First Presidency on June 25, 1833. [36] However, he later learned in another revelation that the New Jerusalem will have a far more elaborate design than that of the basic Zion cities which he previously had been given. He therefore changed the layout in a new format that would accommodate the requirements of the New Jerusalem.

One of the significant changes was the fact that the temple complex of the New Jerusalem will require forty-five acres instead of four acres as prescribed for the temple at the Zion city of Adam-ondi-Ahman. [37]

Furthermore, Joseph Smith was told that there would be twenty-four temples at the New Jerusalem instead of one. These additional "temples" seem to be sacred administrative structures for the secular management of the various nations throughout the world. [38]

THE RETURN OF THE TEN TRIBES

Undoubtedly the most important single event to occur at the New Jerusalem before the Second Coming will be the return of the lost ten tribes from "the land of the north." The scripture says:

"And they who are in the north countries shall come in remembrance before the Lord; and their prophets shall hear his voice, and shall no longer stay themselves; and they shall smite the rocks, and the ice shall flow down at their presence.

"And an highway shall be cast up in the midst of the great deep. Their enemies shall become a prey unto them,

"And in the barren deserts there shall come forth pools of living water; and the parched ground shall no longer be a thirsty land.

"And they shall bring forth their rich treasures unto the children of Ephraim, my servants. And the boundaries of the everlasting hills shall tremble at their presence. And there shall they fall down and be crowned with glory, even in Zion, by the hands of the servants of the Lord, even the children of Ephraim. And they shall be filled with songs of everlasting joy.

"Behold, this is the blessing of the everlasting God upon the tribes of Israel, and the richer blessing upon the head of Ephraim and his fellows. And they also of the tribe of Judah, after their pain shall be sanctified in holiness before the Lord, to dwell in his presence day and night, forever and ever." [39]

This extremely enlightening scripture tells us a multitude of things. For example:

1. Here, as in other passages, the Lord refers to the lost ten tribes as "those in the north countries." In one passage, the Lord specifically speaks of the "TEN TRIBES from the land of the north." [40]

2. It says these people, wherever they are, have God's prophets among them, and the Lord will speak to them. All of this implies the existence of the ten tribes as a distinct people isolated somewhere out there in God's great domain, and they are being prepared for their great migration to Zion. A specific reference to this migration was made by Joseph Smith during a conference in June, 1831. He stated that:

"John the Revelator was among the ten tribes . . . to prepare them for their return from their long dispersion." [41]

This also clearly implies a separate and distinct people.

3. The warring nations will first become aware of the ten tribes when they begin smashing their way through the arctic mountains. It says the rocks will go crashing down before them and the ice will melt and flow down in a flood. Obviously, all of this indicates that the ten tribes make their first appearance far north of the inhabitable part of the earth.

4. But how did they get into this freezing, uninhabitable part of the planet? The Lord says they arrived there on a miraculous highway that God "cast up in the midst of the great deep." So this highway ends in the North American arctic among the rocks and ice, but where did it begin? What did the Lord mean by the "great deep"? Is He referring to the depths of the ocean or the depths of outer space? If the Lord is referring to outer space, then perhaps a number of passages of scripture become more meaningful. For example, one scripture says:

"If any of thine be driven out unto the OUTMOST PART OF HEAVEN, from thence will the Lord thy God gather thee, and from thence will he fetch thee." [42]

Then there is the statement of the Savior when He said to His apostles:

"And he shall send his angels with a great sound of a trumpet, and they shall gather together his elect from the four winds, from one end of HEAVEN to the other." [43]

In a modern revelation the Lord said:

"Yea, verily I say unto you again, the time has come when the voice of the Lord is unto you: Go ye out of Babylon; gather ye out from among the nations, from the four winds, from one end of HEAVEN to the other." [44]

Another interesting point is that the scriptures refer to the Jews as being "dispersed," but the ten tribes are referred to as being "outcasts." Isaiah says:

"And he shall set up an ensign for the nations, and shall assemble the OUTCASTS of Israel, and gather together the DISPERSED of Judah from the four corners of the earth." [45]

All of this raises a most interesting question: Since the city of Enoch was taken from the earth and underwent an interplanetary transmigration, might not the same thing have happened to the ten tribes who were taken elsewhere?

5. Notice that the ten tribes will arrive before the Second Coming. The wicked military dictatorship of the Gentiles will have not yet have been destroyed. The scriptures say these military forces will become the "enemies" of the advancing Ten Tribes but these enemies will not be able to stop them. [46]

6. This scripture also says the ten tribes will return just as the great gathering of the Saints is bringing multitudes into the mountain west. For all of them to survive, the great miracle of the water will have to occur. Imagine the situation where the ten tribes bring millions with them and these multitudes will be joined with the millions of gathering Saints. Isaiah says the original body of the Church will scarcely believe that all these new multitudes have changed the Church into a nation. [47] Isaiah says the mountains and hills will tremble with the impact of their massive presence. [48]

7. By the time the ten tribes arrive, the New Jerusalem will be built up sufficiently so that it can begin operating as the great capital [49] from which the law will go forth. [50] To the radiant joy of the Church, the ten tribes will bring with them RICH TREASURES to further the work of the Church and decorate the modern City of Zion.

THE TEN TRIBES WILL ALSO BRING WITH THEM THEIR MARVELOUS RECORDS

When the lost ten tribes march down to the New Jerusalem they will have a tremendous story to tell. Here are the highlights of what is known about them.

The ten tribes occupied northern Israel and broke away from Judah and Levi around 900 B.C. However, they were extremely apostate, and Isaiah predicted they would be conquered by the Assyrians. [51] This happened between 723 and 721 B.C. [52] The desolated survivors among the Israelites were settled near the headwaters of the Euphrates River, but not for long.

This was because the Babylonians conquered the Assyrians in 607 B.C. and came up to conquer the remnants near the settlements of the ten tribes in 605 B.C. But the Israelites did not wait for the arrival of the Babylonians. They decided quickly to migrate northward.

The only account of the northward flight of the ten tribes is in the Book of Esdras, which is one of the apocryphal books of the Bible. "Apocryphal" means the origin and authenticity of Esdras hasn't been fully established, yet it sets forth several extremely important points worth considering.

For example, it says the ten tribes REPENTED of their rebellion against God and decided:

". . . they would leave the multitude of the heathen, and go forth into a further country, where NEVER MANKIND DWELT, that they might there KEEP THE STATUTES, which they never kept in their own land." [53]

Most historians assume they scattered out across Asia and lost their identity. [54] However, the Jews have assumed that wherever the ten tribes went, they continue to exist as a united, independent people, and therefore the Jews have prayed continually for their return. [55]

When the ten tribes bring their records with them for us to read, one of the exciting episodes will be the account of what happened when Jesus ministered to them after His resurrection. Jesus told the Nephites that never before had He visited the ten tribes so this was a monumental occasion. [56] That part of the history of the ten tribes may be as amazing as the Savior's visit to the Nephites described in the Book of Mormon.

Another monumental aspect of their history will be a detailed account of where they have been for the last 2,000 or more years, and what happened to provide them with a highway from their homeland to the arctic regions of North America. Jeremiah says that when we hear that story, it will make the crossing of the Red Sea a minor event by comparison. He said:

"Therefore, behold, the days come, saith the LORD, that it shall no more be said, The LORD liveth, that brought up the children of Israel out of the land of Egypt; But, the LORD liveth, that brought up the children of Israel from the land of the north, and from all the lands whither he had driven them: and I will bring them again into their land that I gave unto their fathers." [57]

WHAT ABOUT THE UNITED STATES OF AMERICA?

Now we have two final topics to address before concluding this chapter. The first one is a question:

"What will happen to the United States of America?"

We are told that just as soon as the people adopt God's law, they will be known as "The Kingdom of God."

Of course, the original United States of America will always be remembered with affection and respect as the first free people in modern times, but in view of all the circumstances listed above, it no longer would be appropriate to speak of the United States as anything but a chapter in history.

Notice how appropriate it will be to speak of the new order of things as THE KINGDOM OF GOD. In this new, expansive name, there is no reference to any geographical area, nor will there be any implication of a chauvinistic nature suggesting either racial superiority or regional pride. On the other hand, the royal banner or title of liberty waving over the world under the insignia of the Kingdom of God will be like the ENSIGN spoken of by Isaiah [58] that announces a new righteous dominion that eventually will spread over all the earth.

WHAT ABOUT WASHINGTON, D.C.?

As we already have seen, the Kingdom of God no longer will be limited to its original boundaries of the United States. Therefore, the former capital of Washington, D.C. no longer will be an appropriate center of government. Furthermore, all of the taxes, social services, and administrative controls which formerly centered in Washington, D.C. will be extinct. And since most of the major cities along the Atlantic seaboard will be left in total ruin, there probably will be neither the means nor the motivation to reconstruct the former national capital.

No doubt there will be a deep anxiety to restore the homes of the early patriots—but the beautiful domed capitol with its wings for the Senate and House of Representatives may have lost much of its charm because of the wretched abuse of the people that poured from these halls in those days of corruption when America was burdened by the heaviest debt of any nation on earth, and the people struggled beneath a tax system that was completely outside of the original Constitution.

WHAT ABOUT THE STARS AND STRIPES OR "OLD GLORY"?

The flag of the United States of America has become the symbol of liberty throughout the world. Tens of thousands gave their lives in an attempt to preserve the principles for which it stood. Because of what the original thirteen states accomplished and what the flag came to represent to the whole world, it will have acquired an eternal life.

Therefore, here is what Brigham Young stated on July 8, 1855: "When the day comes in which the Kingdom of God will bear rule, the flag of the United States will proudly flutter unsullied on the flag staff of liberty and equal rights, without a spot to sully its fair surface; the glorious flag our fathers have bequeathed to us then will be unfurled to the breeze by those who have power to hoist it aloft and defend its sanctity." [59]

* * * *

TOPICS FOR REFLECTION AND DISCUSSION

1. As soon as America is cleansed, what are the two things that

will happen very quickly? Who are the two groups of new inhabitants who will come to America? What will temporarily seal off the western hemisphere from the rest of the world?

2. In what region does Isaiah say the new inhabitants who come to America will be inclined to gather? Will they overwhelm the land? Why will the original members of the Church be so amazed?

3. What will change the wilderness of the mountain west into a habitation for millions of people? Why will this be called a miracle? Will the former cities of the wicked Gentiles be refurbished and inhabited?

4. Why will it seem like a miracle to have the people enjoy peace and good order? What kind of culture must be developed among the people to have a society with literally no poverty and no crime? How did both King Benjamin and King Mosiah attain this remarkable level of achievement?

5. What does it mean to share problems "in common"? What do you think are the most important elements to bring about prosperity? Why do you think simplicity is more conducive to a Zion society than complexity?

6. Geographically, what is unique about the location of the site for the New Jerusalem? When it comes time to begin building the New Jerusalem, will masses of people be allowed to swarm toward the spot? Why or why not?

7. Name three things that will be unique about the New Jerusalem. What will be the primary purpose for the conference at Adam-ondi-Ahman? Will the world know about it? Will the general membership of the Church know about it?

8. From what direction will the ten tribes come to the New Jerusalem? Do they come as a body or as scattered immigrants? Who will try to stop them? Will they succeed? What will these tribes bring to the New Jerusalem that will be of great value?

9. Name two things you would like to look up in the history of the ten tribes. After the New Jerusalem is established, what will happen to the United States of America?

10. What is likely to happen to Washington, D.C.? Will the flag of the United States be preserved?

1.   Isaiah 29: 14
2.   1 Nephi 13:30
3.   Matthew 24:15
4.   Revelation 9:16
5.   D&C 45:68–69
6.   Moses 7:62–63
7.   Teachings of Joseph Smith, op. cit., pp. 160-161
8.   Luke 21:25
9.   D& 61:15–16
10. D&C 45:69
11. Isaiah 33:15–16
12. Isaiah 2:2–3
13. Isaiah 35:1-2
14. Isaiah 35:6–7
15. Isaiah 54:2–3
16. *Ensign* magazine, May 1994, p. 21
17. Luke 2:14
18. Isaiah 2:3
19. Mosiah 2:13–14
20. Mosiah 29:14–15
21. *Journal of Discourses*, vol. 11, p. 275
22. Quoted by Hyrum Andrus, *Doctrines of the Kingdom*, Salt Lake City: Bookcraft Publishers, 1973, p. 396
23. George Q. Cannon, *Journal of Discourses*, vol. 26, p. 12
24. *United States Constitution*, Article I, Section 10, clause 1
25. D&C 57:1-3
26. Ernest Lee Tuveson, Redeemer Nation, Chicago: The University of Chicago Press,   1968, p. 129
27. Alvin R. Dyer, *The Refiner's Fire*, Salt Lake City: Deseret Book Company, 1968, p. 91
28. Wilford Woodruff's Journal, vol. 7, p. 422

29. *Journal of Discourses*, vol. 9, p. 270

30. Quoted by Duane S. Crowther, *Prophecy, Key to the Future*, Salt Lake City: Bookcraft Inc., 1962, p. 45

31. Joseph Fielding Smith, Doctrines of Salvation, Salt Lake City: Bookcraft, 1956, vol. 3, p. 13

32. Joseph Fielding Smith, *The Way to Perfection*, Salt Lake City: The Genealogical Society of Utah, 1945, p. 291

33. Daniel 7:9

34. Luke 21:25; D&C 61:14-15

35. Isaiah 2:3

36. Hyrum L. Andrus, *Doctrines of the Kingdom*, Salt Lake City: Bookcraft, Inc., 1973, vol. III, pp. 300-301

37. Ibid., p. 308

38. Ibid.

39. D&C 133:26–35

40. D&C 110:11

41. Joseph Fielding Smith, Essentials of Church History, Salt Lake City:, Deseret News Press, 1922, p. 126.

42. Deuteronomy 30:4

43. Matthew 24:31

44. D&C 133:7

45. Isaiah 11:12

46. D&C 133:28

47. Isaiah 49:20-21

48. D&C 133:27-31

49. 3 Nephi 21:23-26

50. Isaiah 2:3

51. Isaiah, chapter 5; see Skousen, *Isaiah Speaks to Modern Times*, pp. 177 ff.

52. See Skousen, The Fourth Thousand Years, p. 497

53. 2 Esdras 13:41-42

54. Emil G. Kraeling, *Rand McNally Bible Atlas*, pp. 297-298

55. Alfred Edersheim, *The Life and Times of Jesus the Messiah*, Grand Rapids, Mich.: Wm. B. Eerdmans Publishing Co., 1962, p, 78

56. 3 Nephi 17:4

57. Jeremiah 16:14–15

58. Isaiah 11:12

59. Journal of Discourses, vol. 2, p. 317

CHAPTER THREE

THE AMAZING
TENTH ARTICLE OF FAITH

While residing in Nauvoo, Joseph Smith learned that a "Mr. Barstow" was writing a history of New Hampshire, and he had become very interested in the fact that Joseph Smith and his parents had lived in that state for several years, beginning in 1811. Mr. Barstow therefore became anxious to obtain a sketch of the life of Joseph Smith.

Mr. Barstow approached John Wentworth, editor and owner of the Chicago Democrat, to see if he could induce Joseph Smith to write up an account of his early life as well as his beliefs as head of the new Church of Jesus Christ of Latter-day Saints. [1]

As a result of this request, Joseph Smith wrote what has become known as the famous Wentworth Letter. In this document, Joseph Smith recorded for the first time a formal account of his early life. He also set forth a remarkably concise statement of his beliefs, which later became known as "The Articles of Faith." [2]

In this chapter, we will discuss the contents of the tenth article of faith which covers a kaleidoscopic vision of the future that is totally astonishing—especially when we analyze each part of it.

Here is the amazing tenth article of faith:

WE BELIEVE IN THE LITERAL GATHERING OF ISRAEL AND IN THE RESTORATION OF THE TEN TRIBES; THAT ZION WILL BE BUILT UPON THE AMERICAN CONTINENT; THAT CHRIST WILL REIGN PERSONALLY UPON THE EARTH; AND, THAT THE EARTH WILL BE RENEWED AND RECEIVE ITS PARADISIACAL GLORY.

It will be observed that we have already discussed three of these great events mentioned in this article of faith. They are as follows, in the order of their sequence:

1. The literal gathering of Israel which takes place right after the cleansing of America.

2. That Zion will be built upon the American continent. This occurs after the gathering of Israel when America is sealed off by roaring seas so that it cannot be reached by sail or plane. In this isolated condition, the scripture says Zion cities will be built and it will be the only part of the earth where peace will prevail.

3. The lost ten tribes will be restored while Gog and his huge army and dictatorship are built up. After the Battle of Armageddon, the Savior will rescue the Jews and convert them to Christianity.

The righteous then are caught up to meet the Savior as He appears to all mankind. A consuming fire then sweeps the wicked from the earth as seen by Malachi, and the earth then is renewed and elevated to its paradisiacal glory. The scriptures have a lot to say about this marvelous transition that will return the earth to the region of its creation and rearrange the entire tectonic structure of the surface of the earth. Here is the sequence of events.

THE JEWS BUILD THEIR TEMPLE IN JERUSALEM

If we are reading the sequence of these prophetic events accurately, it would appear that while America is sealed off and building her Zion cities, the tribe of Judah will be gathering from all over the war-torn world to seek safety in their traditional homeland surrounding Old Jerusalem.

By this time, circumstances will have permitted the Jews to build their fourth temple. This is the temple seen by Ezekiel in vision [3] and the one to which the Savior will come.

The three previous temples—the one built by Solomon around 950 B.C., the one built by Zerubbabel around 516 B.C., and the one built by Herod at the time of Christ—all were destroyed, and while this fourth temple will be attacked, it will continue to survive right into the Millennium.

As this beautiful edifice is built up to crown the heights of Mount Moriah, no doubt Gog—the prince of the Gentiles—will be watching as the Jews gather their wealth from all over the world to beautify Jerusalem and make this temple the most elaborate "house of the Lord" ever constructed.

THE COMING OF THE TEN TRIBES

A short time after the Kingdom of God is established in America and the New Jerusalem has become its new capital, the hosts of the lost ten tribes suddenly will make their appearance in the north.

They will come pouring forth across a miraculous highway which terminates in the North American arctic. However, Gog, the prince of the Gentiles, will be setting up his vast military dictatorship and will resist the ten tribes. But this vast host of Israelites somehow will sweep down past this opposition and continue on their trek to the New Jerusalem where they can receive their endowment in the temples of God. [4]

The ten tribes will bring their riches to embellish the New Jerusalem with yet greater beauty, [5] and they will bring precious records that describe in detail what happened to them after they became "lost." [6]

All this will be so marvelous that the people of the world will no longer tell their children about the crossing of the Red Sea in the days of Moses, but will tell them the far more exciting story of the ten tribes crossing over the great gulf on their miraculous highway that ended in arctic America and allowed them to march on to Zion. [7]

THE BATTLE OF ARMAGEDDON

While the ten tribes are attending to their ordinances in the temples of Ephraim, [8] the great battle of Armageddon at Jerusalem probably will take place. We assume the western hemisphere still will be sealed off, and if that is the case, the building of Zion cities will continue and the Kingdom of God on the western hemisphere won't be involved when the siege of Jerusalem begins and the Battle of Armageddon takes place.

It appears that Gog will have conquered much of Europe and Asia before he turns his greedy war machine on the land of Palestine, where the Jews have been gathering with all their wealth. The greed of Gog is specifically referred to by the prophet Ezekiel who quotes Gog as saying:

"I will go up to the land of unwalled villages; I will go to them that are at rest, that dwell safely, all of them dwelling without walls, and having neither bars nor gates,

"To take a spoil, and to take a prey; to turn thine hand upon the desolate places that are now inhabited, and upon the people that are gathered out of the nations, which have gotten cattle and goods, that dwell in the midst of the land." [9]

Notice that Gog will conquer every city in Israel on the way to Jerusalem. John the Beloved says the military might of Gog which will be spreading the "abomination of desolation" all across Europe and Asia will constitute a vast army of 200,000,000. [10]

But at Jerusalem Gog and his mighty host will come to a sudden halt. Two prophets will have been raised up among the Jews with powers unlike anything Gog has seen before. An angel described what these two prophets will be able to do:

"And if any man will hurt them, fire proceedeth out of their mouth, and devoureth their enemies: and if any man will hurt them, he must in this manner be killed. These have power to shut heaven, that it rain not in the days of their prophecy: and have power over waters to turn them to blood, and to smite the earth with all plagues, as often as they will." [11]

For over three years (actually 42 months) these prophets will hold these great gentile armies at bay. [12] But Gog in all his stubborn fury will yet rage against Jerusalem, and in a final burst of diabolical strength, his armies will succeed in killing the two prophets. [13] Then they will slaughter the Jews by the thousands as they make their way toward the temple. By that time, half of the city will have been subjugated. [14]

With triumphant glee, the Gentile monarch orders a brief cease fire to hold a victory banquet and spread the news that the prophets who "tormented" them have been killed. Gog will not permit them to be buried, but will order their bodies to be left lying in the street while he and his generals celebrate in a drunken orgy that will last three-and-a-half days. [15]

But at the end of this period, Gog and his armies will have the most shocking surprise of their lives.

The mutilated bodies of the two prophets suddenly will rise up fully restored. Then a great voice will be heard from heaven saying, "Come up hither," and the two prophets will ascend in a cloud as Gog and his hosts watch in amazement. [16]

Then things really will begin to happen.

Jesus suddenly will appear on the Mount of Olives with a great host, and the scripture says He shall "utter his voice and all the ends of the earth shall hear it." [17] At this point the prophet Zechariah says:

"And his feet shall stand in that day upon the mount of Olives, which is before Jerusalem on the east, and the mount of Olives shall cleave in the midst thereof toward the east and toward the west, and there shall be a very great valley; and half of the mountain shall remove toward the north and half of it toward the south. And ye shall flee to the valley of the mountains. . . .

"And it shall come to pass in that day, that the light shall not be clear, nor dark: But it shall be one day which shall be known to the LORD, not day, nor night: but it shall come to pass, that at evening time it shall be light." [18]

As the Jews gather around their Great Deliverer, it would seem that He withholds His glory as a resurrected being, for they do not appear to have any way of knowing that they are looking at their long-awaited Messiah. In wonderment they ask:

"What are these wounds in thine hands and in thy feet? Then shall they know that I am the Lord; for I will say unto them: These wounds are the wounds with which I was wounded in the house of my friends. I am he who was lifted up. I am Jesus that was crucified. I am the Son of God. And then shall they weep because of their iniquities; then shall they lament because they persecuted their king." [19]

THE FATE OF GOG AND HIS HOSTS

Meanwhile, God's judgment will be descending on the hosts of Gog and Magog. This tidal wave of destruction will be totally devastating. The Lord said to Ezekiel:

"I will rain upon him, and upon his bands, and upon the many people that are with him, an overflowing rain, and great hailstones, fire, and brimstone." [20]

"And I will turn thee back, and leave but the sixth part of thee." [21]

The tens of thousands of the hosts of Gog who will be slain will be a plague on the land of Israel. For months, the people will be laboring by day and by night to bury the dead. Ezekiel writes:

"And it shall stop the noses of the passengers: and there shall they bury Gog and all his multitude: and they shall call it The valley of Hamon–gog.

"And seven months shall the house of Israel be burying of them, that they may cleanse the land. Yea, all the people of the land shall bury them. . . . And they shall sever out men of continual employment, passing through the land to bury with the passengers those that remain upon the face of the earth, to cleanse it: after the end of seven months shall they search." [22]

THE END OF BLOOD SACRIFICES AT THE TEMPLE IN JERUSALEM

The fourth temple in Jerusalem will be copied after the earlier temples of the Jews, and therefore will be designed for blood sacrifices. However, once the Jews have learned that their Messiah has come, the purpose of these blood sacrifices—in anticipation of Christ's sacrifice—will give them a new perspective. Nevertheless, Joseph Smith indicated that the law of sacrifice will be continued as part of the "restitution of all things" until the sons of Levi have learned how to offer these sacrifices "in righteousness." [23]

Such a time was anticipated by John the Baptist when he restored the Aaronic Priesthood and said:

"This [Priesthood of Aaron] shall never be taken again from the earth, until the sons of Levi do offer again an offering unto the Lord in righteousness." [24]

Malachi indicates that the problem for the Levites is not merely learning the ritual in righteousness, but having a corps of humble and righteous Levites who are worthy to perform the ordinances. He says:

"And he shall sit as a refiner and purifier of silver: and he shall purify the sons of Levi, and purge them as gold and silver, that they may offer unto the LORD an offering in righteousness. Then shall the offering of Judah and Jerusalem be pleasant unto the LORD, as in the days of old, and as in former years." [25]

When the Lord is fully satisfied that the "offering of Judah and Jerusalem is pleasant unto the Lord," no doubt He will say to the priesthood in Jerusalem as He did to the priesthood among the Nephites:

"And ye shall offer up unto me no more the shedding of blood; yea, your sacrifices and your burnt offerings shall be done away, for I will accept none of your sacrifices and your burnt offerings. And ye shall offer for a sacrifice unto me a broken heart and a contrite spirit." [26]

When the appropriate time comes, all the higher ordinances can be introduced into the holy precincts of the temple in Jerusalem just as they will be practiced in the New Jerusalem.

THE ERA WHEN CHAOS REIGNS SUPREME IN THE EARTH

When the military dictatorship of Gog disintegrates following the Battle of Armageddon, there will be absolute chaos among the people of Asia and Europe.

To make a bad situation totally catastrophic, the surface of the earth will begin to rumble and quake, the oceans will heave beyond their bounds, incurable diseases will break out, and devastation similar to what nuclear war might bring will be waged. Here are some of the scriptural comments concerning this time:

"And after your testimony cometh wrath and indignation upon the people. For after your testimony cometh the testimony of earthquakes, that shall cause groanings in the midst of her, and men shall fall upon the ground and shall not be able to stand. And also cometh the testimony of the voice of thunderings, and the voice of lightnings, and the voice of tempests, and the voice of the waves of the sea heaving themselves beyond their bounds. And all things shall be in commotion; and surely, men's hearts shall fail them; for fear shall come upon all people." [27]

And again:

"And in that generation shall the times of the Gentiles be fulfilled. And there shall be men standing in that generation, that shall not pass until they shall see an overflowing scourge; for a desolating sickness shall cover the land. But my disciples shall stand in holy places, and shall not be moved; but among the wicked, men shall lift up their voices and curse God and die.

"And there shall be earthquakes also in divers places, and many desolations; yet men will harden their hearts against me, and they will take up the sword, one against another, and they will kill one another." [28]

Joel appears to have witnessed nuclear warfare or some other kind of cataclysmic disaster in his vision. He says:

"A great people and a strong; there hath not been ever the like, neither shall be any more after it, even to the years of many generations. A fire devoureth before them; and behind them a flame burneth: the land is as the garden of Eden before them, and behind them a desolate wilderness; yea, and nothing shall escape them." [29]

The following passage suggests both nuclear warfare and nuclear fallout:

"The seed is rotten under their clods, the garners are laid desolate, the barns are broken down; for the corn is withered. How do the beasts groan! the herds of cattle are perplexed, because they have no pasture; yea, the flocks of sheep are made desolate.

"O LORD, to thee will I cry: for the FIRE hath devoured the pastures of the wilderness, and the FLAME hath burned all the trees of the field. The beasts of the field cry also unto thee: for the rivers of waters are dried up, and the FIRE hath devoured the pastures of the wilderness." [30]

THE SEALING OF THE 144,000

It is under these abhorrent conditions that the Lord will undertake to send out His final battalion of missionaries to warn the people that the end has come, and they must either accept the gospel and flee to Zion or they will be sealed up by the priesthood to be destroyed in the impending avalanche of destruction at the time of the Second Coming.

No ordinary band of missionaries could survive this kind of assignment. The Lord therefore plans to send out a contingent of 144,000 young high priests who never have violated their chastity, and who will be sealed up against being killed by their wicked enemies. In other words, they will be like the Three Nephites. John the Beloved saw it and says:

"And I looked, and, lo, a Lamb stood on the mount Sion, and with him an hundred forty and four thousand, having his Father's name written in their foreheads . . . And they sung as it were a new song . . . and no man could learn that song but the hundred and forty and four thousand, which were redeemed from the earth.

"These are they which were not defiled with women; for they are virgins. These are they which follow the Lamb whithersoever he goeth. These were redeemed from among men, being the firstfruits unto God and to the Lamb. And in their mouth was found no guile: for they are without fault before the throne of God." [31]

Twelve thousand will be chosen from each of the twelve tribes. This will include 12,000 from Judah. What a metamorphosis this will be for these young Jews. Only a short time before, these youthful Hebrews would probably have laughed in derision if someone had said they would soon be sent out as Christian missionaries. But the spectacular events at the Battle of Armageddon will have changed all that. In due time, 12,000 young Jews will be taken to the temple and sealed up along with the rest.

The tribe of Joseph will probably have 6,000 from Ephraim and 6,000 from Manasseh.

The 12,000 from each of the other ten tribes no doubt will be almost entirely from the new arrivals who recently came over the miracle highway that crossed the great deep. Without question, that journey will be a thrilling experience, but nothing compared to what is going to happen to them on this new assignment.

When this youthful 144,000 have been chosen and ordained high priests, [32] they will be taken to the temples in Zion for special preparatory training and then to be sealed by a special ordinance so they can endure the dangers of this new assignment. Orson Pratt describes how the 144,000 will be sealed according to his understanding:

"The Lord will purify their bodies until they shall be quickened, and renewed and strengthened, and they will be partially changed, not to immortality, but changed in part that they can be filled with the power of God, and they can stand in the presence of Jesus, and behold his face in the midst of the Temple.

"This will prepare them for further ministrations among the nations of the earth. It prepares them to go forth in the days of tribulation and vengeance upon the nations of the wicked when

God will smite them [those wicked nations] with pestilence, plague, and earthquake, such as former generations never knew.

"Then the servants of God will need to be armed with the power of God, they will need to have that sealing blessing pronounced upon their foreheads that they can stand forth in the midst of these desolations and plagues and not be overcome by them.

"When John the Revelator describes this scene he says he saw four angels sent forth, ready to hold the four winds that should blow from the four quarters of heaven. Another angel ascended from the east and cried to the four angels and said: 'Smite not the earth now, but wait a little while.' How long? 'Until the servants of our God [the 144,000—Rev. 7:3-4] are sealed in their foreheads.' What for? To prepare them to stand forth in the midst of these desolations and plagues, and not be overcome.

"When they are prepared, when they have received a renewal of their bodies in the Lord's temple, and have been filled with the Holy Ghost and purified as gold and silver in a furnace of fire, then they will be prepared to stand before the nations of the earth and preach glad tidings of salvation in the midst of judgments that are to come like a whirlwind upon the wicked." [33]

The physical refinement or translation of the 144,000 sounds almost identical to the physical refinement granted to the three Nephite disciples who wanted to have power over death and to remain on the earth until the Second Coming.

WHAT IT WOULD BE LIKE TO PREACH THE GOSPEL WITHOUT BEING SUBJECT TO DEATH

Not only the Three Nephites, but also John the Beloved made this request to minister among men until the Savior came the second time. We have a description of what it was like for these people to move among the wicked like ordinary people, but not be subject to death. The scripture says:

"And they did cast them into prison; but by the power of the word of God, which was in them, the prisons were rent in twain, and they went forth doing mighty miracles among them. Nevertheless, and notwithstanding all these miracles, the people did harden their hearts, and did seek to kill them, even as the Jews at Jerusalem sought to kill Jesus, according to his word.

"And they did cast them into furnaces of fire, and they came forth receiving no harm. And they also cast them into dens of wild beasts, and they did play with the wild beasts even as a child with a lamb; and they did come forth from among them, receiving no harm.

"Nevertheless, the people did harden their hearts, for they were led by many priests and false prophets to build up many churches, and to do all manner of iniquity." [34]

It would appear from the writings of John the Beloved that the

144,000 young high priests who take the gospel message to every nation, kindred, tongue, and people for the last time, will confront circumstances very much like that of the Three Nephites.

THE TASK OF THE 144,000 TO WARN AND SEAL UP EVERY NATION

In 1832, Joseph Smith was asked:

"What are we to understand by sealing the one hundred and forty–four thousand, out of all the tribes of Israel—twelve thousand out of every tribe?" [35]

He replied:

"We are to understand that those who are sealed are high priests, ordained unto the holy order of God, to administer the everlasting gospel; for they are they who are ordained out of every nation, kindred, tongue, and people, by the angels to whom is given power over the nations of the earth, to bring as many as will come to the church of the Firstborn." [36]

Obviously, any who desire to join the church of the Firstborn will be told to flee to Zion in America. Those who reject the message will be left to the holocaust of destruction which will be sweeping over Europe, Asia, Africa, and the islands of the sea.

There is one passage of scripture which indicates that some of the rampaging militant forces that are spreading the "abomination of desolation" across the earth will try to attack Zion. Something similar happened in the days of Enoch shortly after he set up his Zion society. However, Enoch did not resist these raiders with an army. Instead, he used his priesthood. The scripture says:

"He [Enoch] spake the word of the Lord, and the earth trembled, and the mountains fled, even according to his command; and the rivers of water were turned out of their course; and the roar of the lions was heard out of the wilderness; and all nations feared greatly, so powerful was the word of Enoch, and so great was the power of the language which God had given him.

"There also came up a land out of the depth of the sea, and so great was the fear of the enemies of the people of God, that they fled and stood afar off and went upon the land which came up out of the depth of the sea. And the giants of the land, also, stood afar off; and there went forth a curse upon all people that fought against God." [37]

Perhaps something similar will happen when Zion is attacked in the latter days. But whether powerful armies are sent forth to protect God's people or the prophet of that day uses the powers of the priesthood, the results will be the same. We learn this from the scripture which says:

"And it shall be said among the wicked: Let us not go up to battle against Zion, for the inhabitants of Zion are terrible; wherefore we cannot stand. And it shall come to pass that the righteous shall be gathered out from among all nations, and shall come to Zion, singing with songs of everlasting joy." [38]

PREPARING THE EARTH FOR ITS PARADISIACAL GLORY AND THE SECOND COMING OF CHRIST

The transition that will take place on the face of the planet during the final stages of preparation before the Second Coming of Christ will be a triumph for the Saints and a catastrophe for those who yet remain alive among the wicked. Concerning the righteous, the Lord says:

"And the Saints that are upon the earth, who are alive, shall be quickened and be caught up to meet him." [39]

Concerning the wicked who yet remain upon the earth, the Lord says:

"Last of all, these all are they who will NOT BE GATHERED WITH THE SAINTS, to be caught up unto the church of the Firstborn, and received into the cloud.

"These are they who are liars, and sorcerers, and adulterers, and whoremongers, and whosoever loves and makes a lie . . . These are they who suffer the vengeance of eternal fire." [40]

When Malachi saw the destruction of the wicked who rejected the call of the 144,000, he said:

"For, behold, the day cometh, that shall burn as an oven; and all the proud, yea, and all that do wickedly, shall be stubble; and the day that cometh shall burn them up, saith the Lord of hosts, that it shall leave them neither root nor branch." [41]

The destruction of the wicked apparently occurs while the whole surface of the earth is in convulsions. Jeremiah says:

"I beheld the mountains, and, lo, they trembled, and all the hills moved lightly . . . I beheld, and, lo, the fruitful place was a wilderness, and all the cities thereof were broken down at the presence of the Lord, and by his fierce anger." [42]

All this is to restore the earth to its paradisiacal glory as it existed before it was divided into continents and islands. We read that a voice shall be heard among all the people, saying:

"And it shall be a voice as the voice of many waters, and as the voice of a great thunder, which shall break down the mountains, and the valley shall not be found.

"He shall command the great deep, and it shall be driven back into the north countries, and the islands shall become one land; and the land of Jerusalem and the land of Zion shall be turned back into their own place, AND THE EARTH SHALL BE LIKE AS IT WAS IN THE DAYS BEFORE IT WAS DIVIDED." [43]

THE MIGRATION OF THE EARTH BACK TOWARD KOLOB IN THE CENTER OF OUR GALAXY

It might very well be at this time—while the righteous are "caught up," and the surface of the earth is being restructured— that the whole planet will be pulled out of its orbit around the sun and sent hurtling back across the heavens toward the star cluster around Kolob from whence the earth had its origin. The wrenching of the earth out of its orbit around the sun is referred to by the Lord where he says:

"The earth shall tremble and reel to and fro as a drunken man." [44]

Isaiah saw a vision of this astronomical event and describes what will happen. He says:

"The earth shall reel to and fro like a drunkard, and shall be REMOVED like a cottage." [45]

The Lord said to Isaiah:

"I will shake the heavens, and the EARTH SHALL REMOVE OUT OF HER PLACE . . . And it shall be as the chased roe." [46]

The roe is a small deer which is famous for its speed.

The modern prophets were acquainted with these events. Brigham Young stated:

"When the earth was framed and brought into existence and man was placed upon it, it was near the throne of our father in heaven [which is near Kolob [47]]. And . . . when man fell, the earth fell into space, and took up its abode in this planetary system, and the sun became our light . . . This is the glory the earth came from, and when it is glorified IT WILL RETURN AGAIN UNTO THE PRESENCE OF THE FATHER." [48]

The earth is presently around 30,000 light years away from the center of our galaxy. Many of the largest stars are clustered there, and perhaps this is where Kolob can be found. This would mean that in order for our planet to race back towards Kolob in a reasonable time, it would have to travel faster than the speed of light. Isaiah said the people who survive the cleansing of the earth and actually witness this terrifying event will see the star system where we are now situated "dissolved, and the heavens shall be rolled together as a scroll." [49]

Because the earth will be traveling at such an incredible speed as it races toward Kolob, the stars will undoubtedly look as though they are falling from heaven as the earth sweeps past them. [50]

If Kolob is at the center of that huge cluster of stars that provide so much light for our galaxy, when our earth returns to its home base near Kolob it will be completely surrounded by these great star giants. No doubt this is why John the Revelator says that when the earth settles into its final resting place, there "will be no night there." [51] This condition will exist all during the Millennium.

THE SECOND COMING

At last the earth will be ready for the glorious Second Coming of the Savior. The scripture says:

"And there shall be silence in heaven for the space of half an hour; and immediately after shall the curtain of heaven be unfolded, as a scroll is unfolded after it is rolled up, and the face of the Lord shall be unveiled." [52]

It will be like a trumpet from eternity declaring:

ISRAEL, BEHOLD THY GOD!

* * * *

TOPICS FOR REFLECTION AND DISCUSSION

1. What circumstances unfolded that brought Joseph Smith to write the famous Wentworth letter? Can you name the four prophetic declarations Joseph made in the tenth article of faith?

2. How many temples have the Jews built, and who oversaw their construction? Who will make a surprise visit to the Jews' next temple? For what purpose will the Jews use their temple, and how long will that continue?

3. How will the coming of the lost ten tribes help build the New Jerusalem? What precious treasures will they bring with them? Why do you think their return will outshine the crossing of the Red Sea by Moses?

4. When the great armies of Gog lay waste to Israel and prepare to destroy Jerusalem, what great force for good will stop them in their tracks? How long will those gentile armies be held back? What ultimately happens to break the stalemate? What becomes of the two prophets?

5. Who arrives on the scene just as Gog and his armies sweep across Jerusalem? What does this leader do for the Jews at the Mount of Olives? What physical feature reveals who this great leader is? How will the Jews respond?

6. Why will the Jews continue offering blood sacrifices at their new temple in Jerusalem, even after Jesus makes His appearance? When the sons of Levi have satisfied the Lord's requirements at the temple, what new offering will He ask of them?

7. When Gog and his dictatorship are destroyed, what will cause chaos to break out in the freed lands? What added troubles are prophesied to torment these lands after Gog is removed?

8. What attributes will each of the specially chosen 144,000 servants of the Lord have in common? From where will these 144,000 be selected? Where will these servants be sent, and what kind of landscape and environment will be awaiting them? What is their specific task?

9. According to Isaiah, Abraham, and statements by the Lord, what appears to be the earth's destiny after it has undergone its cleansing and the righteous are "caught up"? According to one theory, where might Kolob be found, and how far from us is that right now?

10. How many of the four prophetic declarations in the tenth article of faith do you see fulfilled or starting to be fulfilled today?

1. B. H. Roberts, *The History of the Church*, vol. 2, pp. 130-131
2. Ibid.
3. Ezekiel, chapter 41
4. D&C 133:32
5. D&C 133:30
6. 3 Nephi 29:12-14
7. Jeremiah 16:14-15
8. D&C 133:32
9. Ezekiel 38:11–12
10. Revelation 9:16
11. Revelation 11:5–6
12. Revelations 11:2-3
13. Revelation 11:7-8
14. Zechariah 14:2
15. Revelation 11:10
16. Revelation 11:11-12
17. D&C 45:49
18. Zechariah 14:6–7
19. D&C 45:51–53
20. Ezekiel 38:22
21. Ezekiel 39:2
22. Ezekiel 39:11–14
23. *Teachings of Joseph Smith*, pp. 172-173
24. D&C 13:1
25. Malachi 3:3–4
26. 3 Nephi 9:19–20
27. D&C 88:88–91
28. D&C 45:30–33
29. Joel 2:2–3
30. Joel 1:17–20
31. Revelation 14:1–5
32. D&C 77:11
33. *Journal of Discourses*, vol. 15:365-366
34. 4 Nephi 1:30–34
35. D&C 77:11
36. D&C 77:11

37. Moses 7:13–15
38. D&C 45:70–71
39. D&C 88:96
40. D&C 76:102-105
41. Malachi 4:1
42. Jeremiah 4:24-26
43. D&C 133:22-24
44. D&C 88:87; 45:48
45. Isaiah 24:20
46. Isaiah 13:13–14
47. Abraham 3:3
48. *Journal of Discourses* vol. 17:143
49. Isaiah 34:4
50. Ibid.; D&C 29:14; 34:9; 45:52; 88:87
51. Revelation 22:5
52. D&C 88:95

CHAPTER FOUR

SEVEN STEPS
IN SETTING UP
GOD'S LAW

Having traced the predicted unfolding of events between now and the Second Coming, let us now go back and examine more closely the means by which a Zion society is administered. The most important feature is the setting up of God's law. This can be done after (1) there has been a cleansing of the land, (2) the raising up of a virtuous people, and (3) the restoration of the original Constitution.

As we discussed in an earlier publication—The Majesty of God's Law—the American Founding Fathers knew about the prophecy of Moses that in the latter days the remnants of Israel would begin to gather together and once more set up the divine law that God had revealed to Moses. [1]

We therefore go back to the Bible to remind ourselves how the Lord told Moses to organize the people so they could practice God's law.

STEP ONE—TAKE A CENSUS OF THE PEOPLE BY FAMILIES

It will be recalled that Moses was told that the first step was to divide and number the people by families. [2] However, only men over twenty years of age were to be counted in this official census because it was designed to measure the military strength of Israel as well as the means of governing the people. [3]

We often hear it said that the family is the "basic unit of society," but only under God's law was the family treated as the basic undergirding political and social unit of the whole NATION. Perhaps the term "family" should be defined. Here is the Lord's definition:

"But from the beginning of the creation God made them male and female. For this cause shall a man leave his father and mother, and cleave to his wife; and they twain shall be one flesh: so then they are no more twain, but one flesh. What therefore God hath joined together, let no man put asunder." [4]

Once a man and woman have been joined together in sacred marriage, they (together with their children, when they arrive) comprise a family.

Notice that a single individual is not a "family" under God's law. Single individuals remain part of the family of his or her parents until they set forth and structure a unit of their own.

Neither does a liaison between two homosexual males or two lesbian females constitute a family. Among the ancient pagan societies such as Greece and Rome, these relationships became acceptable, but God and His servants always have described these perversions of human relationships as an "abomination." [5]

STEP TWO—DIVIDE THEM INTO TENS, FIFTIES, HUNDREDS, AND THOUSANDS

Having numbered the entire population by families, the second step was to divide them into a hierarchy of small, self-governing groups. Here is the way Moses was told to do it:

"Moreover thou shalt provide out of all the people able men, such as fear God, men of truth, hating covetousness; and place such over them, to be rulers of thousands, and rulers of hundreds, rulers of fifties, and rulers of tens:

"And let them judge the people at all seasons: and it shall be, that every great matter they shall bring unto thee, but every small matter they shall judge: so shall it be easier for thyself, and they shall bear the burden with thee." [6]

When Moses had done this, he must have been amazed to see how simple it was to manage the affairs of the people. Suddenly he had about 78,000 assistants to help him. This is easily calculated from the following:

The Bible says there were a little over 600,000 adults available for military service and eligible for administrative responsibilities. [7] When Moses divided these into units of tens, it gave him 60,000 elected captains over these units. And when he divided these 600,000 heads of families into fifties, it gave him 12,000 more captains presiding over the units of fifty.

Finally, he was told to divide these 600,000 heads of families into units of a hundred, and that gave him 6,000 additional captains. This adds up to 78,000 elected captains—examined and certified by Moses after their election [8]—to carry the burden of providing for the defense and the efficient administration of three million people.

The marvel of this system is that it will work for ten million or a hundred million.

STEP THREE—DIVIDE THE PEOPLE INTO WARDS OR COMMUNITIES OF A HUNDRED FAMILIES

It turns out that one of the most important aspects of God's law was structuring the people into small, manageable, self-governing units.

The Founders picked up some of these details by studying the Anglo-Saxons. They found that down through the centuries, the

Anglo-Saxons appeared to be the only people who had tried to follow God's pattern of government as given to Moses.

Of course, Thomas Jefferson and many of the other Founders already had become intrigued with the promise of Moses that God's law would be restored in the latter days, and practiced according to the principles that had been revealed from Mount Sinai. [9] To the Founders, this made a study of the Anglo-Saxons highly important. Jefferson went to the trouble of learning the Anglo-Saxon language so he could study their laws in the original text and acquire a deeper insight into just how this system operated. [10]

He especially was impressed with the way the Anglo-Saxons followed the Mosaic formula by dividing their families into tens, fifties, hundreds, thousands, etc. He also found out that the basic community of the Anglo-Saxons was 100 families called a "ward," or a "guarded" and watched-over place. [11] When God restored His church in modern times He also followed the "ward" system, so we assume it was not the Anglo-Saxons who invented this inspired notion of a model community of a hundred families, but the Lord.

The early settlers of New England copied this system and called each voting community a ward. Jefferson was very impressed by the efficiency of these small basic units of self-government. He therefore wrote to John Adams as follows:

"These wards, called townships in New England, are the vital principle of their governments, and have proved themselves the wisest invention ever devised by the wit of man for the perfect exercise of self-government, and for its preservation." [12]

Jefferson proposed the same system for his own state and hoped it would spread to the entire country. He wrote:

"Among other improvements, I hope they will adopt the subdivision of our counties into wards . . . about six miles square each . . . [similar] to the hundreds of your Saxon [King] Alfred." [13]

The size of the township or ward had to be sufficient for the community itself, as well as the surrounding farms, so it could support around 100 families and still allow everyone to live in the town. Jefferson wrote:

"Divide the counties into wards of such size [six miles square] . . . that every citizen can attend, when called on, and act in person." [14]

Jefferson marveled at the ease with which the feelings of the majority of the people could be ascertained when they were divided into these small, manageable units. He said:

"The mayor of every ward . . . would call his ward together, take the simple yea or nay of its members, convey these to the county court, who would hand on those of all its wards to the proper general authority; and the voice of the whole people would be thus fairly, fully, and peaceably expressed, discussed, and decided by the common reason of the society." [15]

Many other states were trying to get a reading of public opinion by holding mass meetings at the county courthouse or in large district rallies where the noise of partisan politicians and the disruption by local drunks made intelligent discussion extremely difficult.

Furthermore, obtaining a solid consensus of the people almost was impossible to ascertain. By way of contrast, Jefferson praised the quiet efficiency of the ward system where the consensus of the people could accurately be determined in a very short period of time. [16]

CONGRESS AGREES TO DIVIDE ALL PUBLIC LANDS INTO TOWNSHIPS OR WARDS

Of course, many of the original states had not shared the enthusiasm of Jefferson for ward townships. For nearly 150 years they had been going ahead and writing up deeds according to natural boundaries or the borders of land taken over by the earliest settlers.

Nevertheless, Congress realized that a better system had to be established for the vast domains of public lands extending far out into the regions of the unsettled West. They therefore accepted the ideas of Jefferson and the New England patriots to divide these virgin lands into ward townships.

On May 20, 1785, Congress enacted a law that all future surveys of public lands would be laid out in wards or townships six miles square. Each of these townships was to be divided into thirty-six sections, and each of these sections was to be one mile square, comprising 640 acres.

As the United States Public Land Survey progressed, some modest adjustments sometimes were required to accommodate natural barriers, but the overall magnificence of this vast land survey is vividly evident to the thousands of people who fly over the midwest and see stretched out from horizon to horizon a perfect checkerboard of cultivated farmlands, ranches, and homesteads.

JEFFERSON VISUALIZED EACH WARD BECOMING SELF SUFFICIENT AND SELF CONTAINED

Not only was it intended that each of the wards or townships would be self-governing, but each one was to look to its own resources for its progress and development as well as its economic independence. This was "community building" of the highest order, and the way Moses originally designed it. Thomas Jefferson pointed out that each ward should have its own schools under the exclusive control of its own parents. [17] Then he went on to say:

"My proposition had for a further object to impart these wards those portions of self-government for which they are best qualified." [18]

This would include:

"1. An elementary school.

"2. A company of militia, with its officers.

"3. A justice of the peace and constable.

"4. Each ward should take care of their own poor.

"5. Their own roads.

"6. Their own police.

"7. Elect within themselves one or more jurors to attend the courts of justice.

"8. Give in at the Folk-house [town hall] their votes for all functionaries reserved to their election.

"Each ward would thus be a small republic within itself, and every man in the State would thus become an acting member of the common government, transacting in person a great portion of its rights and duties . . . entirely within his competence. The wit of man cannot devise a more solid basis for a free, durable, and well administered republic." [19]

Jefferson called these small, solid, self-governing wards "the keystone of the arch of our government," [20] and stated that if each community conscientiously performed its assigned tasks, not only would it become a prosperous, independent entity, but it would leave very little for the counties to worry about. [21]

THE INTERNAL STRUCTURE OF A WARD

Both Moses and the Anglo-Saxons provided us with a detailed account of the way a ward should be structured internally.

Each group of ten families should elect a leader whose name then would be submitted to the chief executive of the ward for approval. Among the Anglo-Saxons, this leader of ten families was appropriately called a Tithing Man—meaning a leader of ten.

Five of these groups of ten then would combine to elect a leader of fifty families—a Vil Man. Since the community consisted of around 100 families, there would be two Vil Men for each ward. The entire community (or village) of 100 families then would combine to elect their chief executive, or Hundred Man, as the Anglo-Saxons called him.

Notice how tight the administrative structure of each ward turned out to be. The Hundred Man had two Vil Men to assist him, and each of the Vil Men had five Tithingmen to assist them. A juvenile delinquent would have a slim chance of hooliganizing a neighborhood for long in this kind of setup!

Of course, the ward was part of a tightly integrated network of other wards comprising the county, and each of the wards was involved in electing the superintendent of the county. The same was true in electing the governor of the state or the officers of the nation. It was a hierarchy of carefully selected public servants, and all were elected into office by the expressed approval of the people at each level.

No wonder Jefferson saw the genius of this inspired political system revealed to Moses and copied by the Anglo-Saxons.

In case of a disaster or emergency, there was an automatic device which a virtuous people always would put into immediate operation. It was called volunteerism. Compassionate people operating on a volunteer basis always have provided more speedy and efficient help than the slow, expensive bureaucracy of a central government.

It is important to understand the principles we mention here because they will be implemented right after the cleansing of America. The survivors will be expected to know how to put the principles of God's law into operation, just as Moses predicted. [22]

STEP FOUR—SETTING UP A SYSTEM OF JUDGES OR CAPTAINS UNDER GOD'S LAW

The next element of God's law—which is remarkably unique— is the way the judiciary is set up to achieve the highest possible quality of justice. Disputes and charges against offenders were handled by the captains or judges over the tens, fifties, hundreds, etc. How these captains or judges decided each case is interesting.

To begin with, there is no reference to lawyers, which happens to be this writer's own profession. The judges did not rely on adversarial arguments of legal orators to reach their conclusions. They were required by God to do their own investigating [23] and then pronounce a judgment which they rendered as surrogates of God himself, and that means they risked the wrath of God if they were dilatory in their investigation or biased in their decree.

It will be recalled that the people were allowed to nominate their own judges—or "captains"—but they had to be approved by the chief executive of the people. Moses left no doubt as to the quality of nominees that he wanted sent up for approval. As we pointed out earlier:

They must be "wise men." [24]

They must be men of proven ability. [25]

They must be men who fear God. [26]

They must be known as men of truth. [27]

They must hate covetousness. [28]

They must be well known among the people. [29]

INSTRUCTIONS TO THE JUDGES

Once the judges were selected and approved, Moses was told to give them very specific instructions as they undertook to provide righteous judgment as official surrogates of the Lord.

They must be willing to hear the complaints of all men and women, small and great, even strangers. [30]

They must judge righteously, according to the circumstances, and fear no man regardless of his status in the community. [31]

They must accept no gifts or favors from anyone, for these blind the eyes of the wise—even judges. [32]

The judges are responsible for conducting their own investigation and getting the facts for themselves. [33]

They must not "wrest" or pervert a true judgment, for "the judgment is God's." This means that the judge is acting as an administrator of God's law and will be held accountable for the righteousness of his judgment. [34]

The judges must insist on two or more witnesses for each offense. These could include witnesses of circumstantial evidence. [35]

Concerning a witness who commits perjury and is therefore a "false" witness, "ye shall do unto him as he had thought to do unto his brother" with his or her false testimony. [36]

The rule of judgment is that he who hurts must be hurt "without pity" or make full satisfaction to the injured party. But there shall be no satisfaction for murder. [37]

When one deliberately takes the life of another, it cannot be negotiated. The murderer must die. It is this passage which implies that all other offenses can be negotiated, even though the law says "death" may be pronounced for a particular offense if the judges consider it appropriate. For example, the judges need the threat of "death" to enforce banishment in case the offender attempts to return. Many of the offenses with "death" as an ultimate penalty were to enforce banishment for those who were corrupting God's Zion society. [38]

When a judge considered a case "too hard" for him, he could appeal it to a higher judge. The party to a case who was not satisfied with the judgment could also appeal. [39]

Decisions of higher judges were to be accepted by lower judges, as well as the parties involved in the case. Insurrection against the judges was a capital offense. [40]

GUIDELINES FOR THE ADMINISTRATION OF JUSTICE

The philosophical object of each judgment was not revenge, but rather to restore the victim or offended party to his original position as far as humanly possible. As we already have pointed out, this was not possible in the case of murder, and therefore, the penalty was automatically death. However, in all other cases, the judges could decree whatever was necessary to achieve a balance of genuine justice.

This was usually done by requiring the offender to provide compensation for injuries, the cost of treatment, the loss of time at his employment, the judge's evaluation of damages for pain and suffering, and any further damages appropriate to the circumstances. Punitive damages also could be added to discourage the offender from similar offenses in the future. [41] As we have mentioned, none of the fines or damages went to the court or the government. Everything was awarded to the victim. [42]

For offenses other than criminal homicide, the penalties could be any of the following:

Fines or damages. [43]

Confiscation of property. [44]

Whipping. However, this was done in the presence of the judge to prevent abuse and would not be equated with "flogging," which was brutal and sometimes life-threatening. [45]

Imprisonment.[46]

Banishment with the threat of death if the offender returned. [47]

As a final note, we should observe the provision that judgments were to be carried out "speedily." [48]

STEP FIVE—MAKE CERTAIN EVERYONE KNOWS THE LAW

The Lord told Moses that His purpose in revealing the code of divine law was so that it could be taught to all the people. He said:

"Come up to me into the mount, and be there: and I will give thee tables of stone, and a law, and commandments which I have written; THAT THOU MAYEST TEACH THEM." [49]

Later on, the Lord said:

"I will speak unto thee all the commandments, and the statutes, and the judgments, WHICH THOU SHALT TEACH THEM, that they may do them in the land which I give them to possess it." [50]

There also was an emphatic decree from the Lord to especially concentrate on the teaching of children. He said:

"Thou shalt teach them [the provisions of God's law] diligently unto thy children, and shalt talk of them when thou sittest in thine house, and when thou walkest by the way, and when thou liest down, and when thou risest up." [51]

STEP SIX—PUT THE PEOPLE UNDER COVENANT TO OBEY THE LAW

Having learned the law, the Lord wanted every Israelite of accountable age to enter into a covenant to honor, sustain, and obey the law:

"And Moses came and called for the elders of the people, and laid before their faces all these words which the Lord commanded him. And all the people answered together, and said, All that the Lord hath spoken we will do." [52]

Shortly afterwards, Moses reminded the people:

"This day the Lord thy God hath commanded thee to do these statutes and judgments: thou shalt therefore keep and do them with all thine heart, and with all thy soul. Thou hast avouched [affirmed by a sacred covenant] the Lord this day to be thy God, and to walk in his ways, and to keep his statutes, and his commandments, and his judgments, and to hearken unto his voice." [53]

From the earliest days of American history, the Founders were convinced that there was no safer and sounder approach to the security and mutual happiness of a nation than to have all of the people enter into a solemn agreement with each other, and then covenant before God that they will honor their commitments.

The earliest and perhaps most famous American covenant was the Mayflower Compact, signed November 11, 1620. This solemn covenant was signed under extremely aggravating circumstances. Nevertheless, scholars agree that it was a highly instructive experience.

It will be recalled that the Pilgrims had suffered persecution, imprisonment, poverty, and exile, but they had hoped the good ship Mayflower would take them to northern Virginia where they could establish a colony and live peacefully by themselves.

As it turned out, the Mayflower was not such a stout and sturdy ship as the Pilgrims had expected. In fact, far out to sea, a heavy storm overtook them, and a main beam cracked and threatened to give way. The whole colony would have drowned had not a passenger brought along a huge screw which was used to hold the beam together. Another timber was used to prop it up and keep it in place.

And so the crippled ship continued on its way. It took over two months to cross the North Atlantic, and when they sighted land, they were alarmed to learn that they were hundreds of miles north of where they were authorized to set up a colony.

The Pilgrims had negotiated a contract with the Virginia Company to settle somewhere along the mouth of the Hudson River, which was at the extreme northern boundary of the Virginia charter. Unfortunately, the ship's master would proceed no further, but landed the passengers on the bleak, snow-covered "wilderness" along the shores of what is now Cape Cod, Massachusetts.

To complicate matters, there were certain "strangers" among them who were not Pilgrims, and when they learned what had happened, they began to boast that since the new colony would be an illegal settlement without any powers of authority, they intended to be a law unto themselves.

Being of a rougher cut than the Pilgrims, the leaders immediately saw the possibility of mutiny after they had landed. The Pilgrim leaders therefore determined to put everyone under covenant to sustain and obey the laws adopted by the colony. So far as is known, the "strangers" appear to have signed along with the rest.

It was a historic moment on November 11, 1620, when forty-one of the 102 passengers, representing nearly all of the men in the company, met in the ship's cabin to sign the famous Mayflower Compact. Concerning this event, Samuel Eliot Morrison of Harvard University, comments as follows:

"Brewster, Bradford, Winslow, Standish, and other leaders of the expedition . . . drew up the famous Mayflower Compact, which almost all the adult men signed. Therein they formed a 'civil body politic,' and promised 'all due submission and obedience' to such 'just and equal laws' as the government they set up might pass. This compact, like the Virginia assembly, [the year before] is an almost startling revelation of the capacity of Englishmen in that era for self-government. Moreover, it was the second instance of Englishmen's determination to live in the colonies under a rule of law. We must never forget this; for in colonies of other European nations the will of the prince, or his representative, was supreme." [54]

This little vignette from our early history illustrates the fact that the Founders had rooted in their souls the firm belief that sound government requires a sacred covenant between the people themselves and openly declared before God as their witness. They were particularly impressed by examples in the Bible where the people prospered, both spiritually and temporally, when they had entered a sacred covenant with each other before God, and made this the foundation of their society.

In fact, they were well aware that the Bible itself is the story of such a covenant. The Old Testament was originally called the Book of the Old Covenant and the New Testament was called the Book of the New Covenant. [55] They knew that ancient Israel, as well as the Christians, lost untold blessings because they did not live up to their covenants with God.

STEP SEVEN—THE INDISPENSABLE TASK OF RAISING UP A VIRTUOUS PEOPLE

The most important single lesson to be learned from Old Testament history is the simple fact that God's law will not function except under the disciplined commitment of a virtuous people. Of course, it is assumed that after the devastating cleansing of the Western Hemisphere, the survivors will be so humbled—even terrified—that they will welcome whatever promises to restore law and order and provide them with some degree of security.

The Founders were well aware that a constitutional government of freedom, peace, and prosperity could only be built within a culture of virtuous and God-loving people. Here are some of their statements worth memorizing:

Benjamin Franklin said: "Only a virtuous people are capable of freedom. As nations become corrupt they have more need of masters." [56]

John Adams said: "Our Constitution was made only for a moral and religious people. It is wholly inadequate to the government of any other." [57]

Samuel Adams said: "Neither the wisest constitution nor the wisest laws will secure the liberty and happiness of a people whose manners are universally corrupt." [58]

One of the lamentations of the Founders was that they were unable to raise up a people sufficiently virtuous and righteous to accommodate the requirements for God's Law.

Of course, the same thing was true of Israel.

The hope of the Founders was that their descendants might someday qualify for the great honor of fulfilling the prophecy of Moses.

THE NAME OF GOD'S NEW WORLD ORDER

Once the people have gone through the seven steps of adopting God's law, the secular name for this great new world order is THE KINGDOM OF GOD.

This great new world order will include all the people of all faiths who recognize and accept the Son of God as the king of kings and covenant to live under His divine law.

Notice that the Kingdom of God is not the Church of God. The first is a secular order for all people. The second is a spiritual order for those who are willing to enter into a somewhat higher plane of service and commitment.

In modern times, it came as a distinct surprise to many people when they learned that the Kingdom of God was not the Church of God.

Perhaps this misunderstanding arose from statements such as the one by Brigham Young when he said that when the Constitution hangs as it were by a single thread, the elders will step forward and save it. [59]

But he was not talking about the Church. He clarified himself later when he said:

"The Kingdom [of God and the Constitution] grows OUT of the Church of Jesus Christ of Latter-day Saints but IT IS NOT THE CHURCH, for a man may be a legislator in that body which will issue laws to sustain the inhabitants of the earth in their individual rights, and still not belong to the Church of Jesus Christ at all." [60]

In other words, after the cleansing of America, the elders of the Church will have done their homework and will know what to do. So will anybody else who has done his homework. The councils of "wise men" throughout the kingdom will include leaders from various faiths, and these comprise the executive branch of the Kingdom of God.

This helps us better understand the original quote by Joseph Smith which Brigham Young was paraphrasing, when Joseph prophesied, "Even this nation will be on the very verge of crumbling to pieces and tumbling to the ground and when the Constitution is upon the brink of ruin this people will be the staff upon which the nation shall lean and THEY shall bear the Constitution away from the very verge of destruction." [61]

* * * *

TOPICS FOR REFLECTION AND DISCUSSION

1. What will be the FIRST step in restoring God's law? How does the Lord define a "family"? What does the Lord say about people of the same sex who try to call themselves a family?

2. What will be the SECOND step in restoring God's law? The Lord said to divide the families into how many different segments? Who selected the captains over each segment? And then who had to give final approval?

3. What will be the THIRD step in restoring God's law? What people did the Founders study to find out more details concerning the actual operation of God's law? What did Thomas Jefferson do so he could study the records of these people?

4. What did these people call a captain of ten? What did they call a captain of fifty? What did they call a captain of a hundred?

About how many assistants did Moses have after he had divided the people according to the Lord's instructions?

5. About how many families constituted a ward? What did this word mean? Why was Jefferson so fascinated with these small units of self-government? Name five of the functions he wanted the wards to handle by themselves.

6. What did Congress do to divide the public lands of the United States into townships and wards? How many sections in each township? How many acres in each section? Why did Jefferson say the heads of families in a township or ward should live in the community and not out on the farm?

7. What will be the FOURTH step in restoring God's law? Will the judges hear lawyers from both sides the way they do today? Who does the investigating to discover the facts?

8. Describe the qualities of the judges under God's law. In making their decisions, whom do they represent? Where human life has been taken with intent to kill, what is the penalty under God's law?

9. What will be the FIFTH step in restoring God's law? Do you think most people really know the law today? Why does the Lord make it mandatory for everyone to learn the law? Then what is the SIXTH step?

10. What will be the SEVENTH step in restoring God's law? Why did the Founders say the entire program will collapse unless this seventh step is permanently established among the people? What is the new name for America after the cleansing?

_____

1. Deuteronomy 30:1-8; Skousen, *The Majesty of God's Law*, chapter 2.

2. Numbers 1:2

3. Numbers 1:3

4. Mark 10:6-9

5. Leviticus 18:22; Romans 1:27; 1 Corinthians 6:9; 1 Timothy 1:10

6.   Exodus 18:21–22

7.   Numbers 1:4,46

8.   Deuteronomy 1:13

9.   Deuteronomy 30:1-8

10. See Skousen, *The Making of America*, pp. 54-61

11. James Hastings, *Dictionary of the Bible*, New York: Charles Scribner's Sons, 1947, vol. 4, p. 896

12. Bergh, *Writings of Thomas Jefferson*, 15:38

13. Ibid. p. 1492

14. Ibid, p. 1399

15. Ibid. p. 1403

16. Ibid. p. 1402

17. Ibid. p. 1379

18. Ibid. p. 1308

19. Ibid. pp. 1492-3

20. Ibid. p. 1309

21. Ibid. p. 1339

22. Deuteronomy 30:1-8

23. Deuteronomy 19:18

24. Deuteronomy 1:11

25. Exodus 18:21

26. Ibid.

27. Ibid.

28. Ibid.

37. Numbers 35:31

38. Deuteronomy 19:21; Numbers 35:31; Ezra 7:26

39. Deuteronomy 1:17

40. Deuteronomy 17:11-2

41. Compare Exodus 22:4 with Exodus 22:1

42. Ibid.

43. Exodus, chapter 22

44. Ezra 7:26

45. Deuteronomy 25:1-3

46. Ibid

47. Ibid.

48. Ibid

49. Exodus 24:12

50. Deuteronomy 5:31

51. Deuteronomy 6:7

52. Exodus 19:7-8

53. Deuteronomy 26:16-17

54. Samuel Eliot Morrison, *The Oxford History of the United States*, New York: Oxford University Press, 1965, p. 55

55. LDS Bible Dictionary, under "Bible"

56. W. Cleon Skousen, *The Making of America*, Washington, D.C.: The National Center for Constitutional Studies, 1985, p. 53.

57. Ibid.

58. Ibid.

59. *Journal of Discourses*, vol 2, p. 182

60. Ibid., vol. 2, p. 310

61. Words of Joseph Smith, Ehat and Cook, p. 416

CHAPTER FIVE

A DUAL ECONOMIC SYSTEM UNDER GOD'S LAW

As the people are organized into wards and trained under God's law, there will be a dual economic structure in operation.

The restored Constitution will allow the general economy to operate on the basis of an honest, free enterprise, competitive economy. However, under the protection of the Constitution, it also will be possible to allow Zion cities to be built. In other words, there will be two separate cultures operating side by side.

THE FREE ENTERPRISE CULTURE UNDER GOD'S LAW

Under a rather ideal system of Adam Smith's concept of free enterprise, the primary emphasis will be on "freedom to choose." This means regulatory ordinances will be minimal.

The object is to have an efficient, orderly society, but with a virtuous people practicing the Golden Rule. In this cultural climate, both buyer and seller walk away from an exchange better off than when they came. For example, a man wants to sell a vehicle and sets the price, with a reasonable margin of profit. At that price the buyer feels he gets a good deal for his money and goes away happy. In that sense, both buyer and seller make a profit.

They each have improved their economic position to meet their respective needs.

Of course, it is natural for the buyer and seller each to come to the bargaining table with a different perspective. The seller may think the vehicle is worth a little more, and the buyer may think the vehicle should cost a little less. In the bargaining process, Adam Smith said, one must always make allowance for a reasonable margin of difference which can be negotiated and still be within the parameters of an honest, just, and acceptable deal by both parties.

The Money System Based On Gold And Silver

The money system will be based on precious metal. However, since metal money is inconvenient to handle in any large quantity, the people may want paper currency for convenience. If the government issues a form of paper currency, it must be redeemable in precious metal on demand.

Some have questioned whether or not there is enough precious metal in existence to sustain a world monetary system, but this was not a problem in the mind of Brigham Young. He said: "I know where there is plenty of gold in these mountains," [1] but then he prayed it would not be discovered lest it divert the people from their immediate task, which was "not to hunt gold but build up the kingdom of God." [2]

When precious metal is fairly plentiful, it maintains a rather steady value based on the cost of mining from the ground and refining at the mint. If the price starts going up for either gold or silver, enterprising people go out and find some more and the price stabilizes again. This, of course, assumes that the money system is not in the hands of bankers or manipulators who can exercise an artificial control over the value of precious metal.

Gold in our own day has fluctuated from $100 an ounce to more than $1,000 an ounce, and silver has fluctuated from $4.50 to more than $40 an ounce. But this wild gyration of prices was manipulated by those who wanted to profit from the fluctuation of the market. Under God's law, the price will be determined by the cost of mining and refining without any profit-taking by monopolists.

THE BANKING SYSTEM

Joseph Smith recommended that the national banking system should be assigned to the national government with branch banks in each of the states. One percent of the interest is usually sufficient to pay for the operation of the bank and the remainder of the profits from interest on loans will be turned over to the general fund to cut down on taxes. In the same way, each of the state banks will be allowed to use any of their profits to cut back on state taxes. This plan was suggested by Joseph Smith in his "Views of the Powers and Policies of the Government of the United States." [3]

Except for interest-free loans to help the poor build a home or meet some emergency, all loans should be made only on the basis of the customer's deposits or a lien on solid collateral. People seeking loans on any other basis can work through a private bank or loan agency that charges higher interest because of the higher risk. However, private banks should not be insured by the government and therefore would work out their own insurance protection to cover liabilities.

Private banks would operate under state charters but could not charge more than a certain amount of interest—usually 10%.

INSURANCE COMPANIES

Pooling the risk for life insurance, fire insurance, accident insurance, disability, retirement, etc., will be on a competitive basis, but companies will be monitored to protect investors.

THE LAW AND ACCOUNTING PROFESSIONS

There will be a new judicial system with righteous judges conducting careful investigations and rendering prompt decisions.

Under God's law, lawyers are not allowed to represent clients in criminal and tort cases. After the judges have determined the facts and then consulted with the offender or the parties to a dispute, most cases can be disposed of rather quickly.

However, a different situation arises in criminal cases where the offender demands a jury trial. In a trial by jury, it is a basic rule that the jury has the right to determine BOTH the law and the facts. This means that if—in this particular case—the law is being applied in an unjust manner, the jury can declare the defendant "not guilty" even though there may have been a technical violation.

The well-known historian Will Durant describes a case during the days of Oliver Cromwell in the 1600s. He writes:

"Four writers were tried . . . that drew thousands of people about the court. Lilburne [the principal offender] challenged the judges, and appealed to the jury. When all four were acquitted there went up from the crowd such a loud and unanimous shout as is never heard in Guildhall, which lasted for about half an hour without intermission." [4]

The Founders thought this power of the jury to determine both the justice of law, as well as the facts of the case, to be a citizen's greatest safety net to protect his freedom and his rights. [5]

John Jay, the first chief justice of the Supreme Court, explained this power to his juries before they retired to make their decisions. He would point out that the judge might give the jury his interpretation of the law but emphasized that it was the right of the jury to interpret and apply the law in a particular case according to their own best sense of justice. [6]

Another improvement in the judiciary under God's law will be streamlining and simplifying the legal procedure, both during the investigation and the later handling of the trial. Because of the corruption of the criminal justice system in our own day, many technicalities have been added which would not be necessary or desirable with an honest, virtuous people. These burdensome encumbrances will be eliminated under God's law.

Lawyers will serve as investigators for the judges and constitute legal facilitators for deeds, wills, contracts, etc. They will also serve as negotiators for major projects undertaken by the government, the states, or by private parties.

Accountants will serve as the principal means of maintaining accountability and credibility in all phases of business and government.

HEALTH CARE

Each ward or perhaps two wards will have their own clinic, and a group of wards or a county will provide a hospital. Both clinics and hospitals will be operated by the doctors serving the area, but the cost of building the facilities will be borne by the community.

The principle of volunteerism will function as it did before the government intruded into health care. Doctors will charge regular patients a reasonable fee and donate a certain percentage of their time caring for any person whom some doctor has certified to be in need of non-compensatory medical attention. The honor and pride of the profession will be based on the quality of preventive medicine and the care of the poor which it provides in that particular county or ward.

Individuals of means will be solicited to donate the funds needed for expensive, sophisticated equipment and also for the support of medical and dental schools in that region.

EDUCATION

Parents will be considered primarily responsible for the education of their children. They also will be responsible for the quality of the curriculum and the selection of textbooks.

The selection and supervision of teachers will be the responsibility of a qualified committee functioning on the ward level for the lower grades and on the county level for the upper grades.

All institutions of learning will emphasize the five basic spiritual values on which constitutional government is founded:

1. The worship and recognition of human dependency on the Creator.

2. The importance of practicing the moral code for happy living revealed by the Creator.

3. Recognizing that approval of the Creator depends upon the way we treat our fellow men.

4. Emphasizing that we will live beyond this life.

5. Emphasizing that we will be judged in the next life according to the way we lived in this one.

Colleges granting an Associate Degree will be maintained according to population needs in a particular region and one or more universities granting advanced degrees will serve the state.

Each county—or association of counties—will provide a technical school for mechanical, engineering, and crafts training.

Private schools and colleges, including home schooling, will be encouraged.

There will be no separate schools for the needy or underprivileged children. It will be the responsibility of the ward and county to see that all children have an equal opportunity to attend the regular schools.

ENVIRONMENTAL PROTECTION, SANITATION, AND MASTER PLANNING

The curse of modern cities is their congestion—too many people crammed together in too little space. This means too much garbage, too much sewage, too much immorality, too much disease, not enough schools, not enough jails, not enough doctors, but an overwhelming quantity of taxes and regulations.

God's law allows for no megalopolis communities. Each community has carefully planned population limits, and a division must occur under the leadership of the county or region as soon as an area begins to become congested.

In the city of Enoch with its divinely inspired layout, the entire community was only one square mile with a surrounding area of six miles square for farms and stock. This meant that it was intended to accommodate only twenty to thirty thousand people. The modern instructions that went with this inspired plan said:

"When this square is thus laid off and supplied, lay off another in the same way, and so fill up the world . . . THIS [meaning all of these little townships combined] is the City of Zion." [7]

This means that the City of Enoch and the City of Zion are not referring to a single community but to a nation.

Setting up a Zion city—based on God's law—requires a very special caliber of people. It is not easy, but it is very rewarding. It worked for Enoch until he and his people were "taken" after 365 years [8] and it worked for the Christians in America for around 200 years. [9] It also worked for the Apostles in Jerusalem until persecution scattered them abroad. [10] It has worked successfully for other groups, some of which eliminated both poverty and crime within a very short period of time. [11]

THE ADVANTAGES OF A ZION SOCIETY

In a modern setting, consider the advantages of a Zion society. Each family will have:

1. A home and a garden without a mortgage.

2. A pleasant, challenging work assignment.

3. High-quality, universal education.

4. Free unemployment insurance.

5. Free disability insurance.

6. Free accident insurance.

7. Free health insurance.

8. Built-in private social security with guaranteed retirement benefits.

ADMINISTERING A ZION SOCIETY

Based on the information now available, here is the way a body of virtuous people can establish a community based on the stewardship principle WHEN GOD HAS AUTHORIZED IT.

1. First and foremost, a Zion society requires a deeply loved and trusted leader. It must be someone who has acquired extensive knowledge of the administrative principles involved in setting up a wide variety of stewardships.

2. The plan requires that the bishop, captain, or president of the "order" be supported by a council of "wise and just" persons. This council is responsible for helping their leader in the distribution of stewardships and performing certain additional tasks such as determining the amount of dividends to be paid out when the community prospers.

3. As for membership in the group, if an individual and his family want to join the group, that individual offers to the group leaders all the property he owns. However, he does not turn the property over to them until there is an agreement on two items:

First, they must indicate to the applicant what they have in mind for his assignment or stewardship and see if it is acceptable to him.

Second, they must tell him how much they are deeding back to him for the operation of the stewardship and the maintenance of his family. When the final arrangements are mutually satisfactory to both the applicant and the leaders of the group, the deed is written up, and he is admitted as a member.

4. The applicant then enters into a sacred and solemn covenant to treat his stewardship (which is legally his) as the property of the Lord. His commitment is to make it as profitable and useful as he can so that the community will know he is a genuine asset to the group. Of course, some stewardships will be in terms of public service rather than profit. This would include such things as teaching, serving as an accountant, technician, or administrator for the group, serving in connection with any of the healing arts, etc. The "profitability" of such a stewardship would be graded on the quality of the service rendered rather than the profit factor.

Such a person would be granted an adequate income to cover his living expenses.

5. At the end of the year, the parable of the talents goes into effect. Those who have been farming, ranching, building, or otherwise engaged in a profitable occupation will turn in to the treasurer of the group everything he has made, except the amount needed for the operation of his stewardship and the expenses of his family. In other words, he retains "according to his wants and his needs, inasmuch as his wants are just." [12] This educational process of developing each member into a profitable servant—who will sacrifice the surplus fruits of his labor for the good of the group— is the key to the amazing prosperity of a Zion society when it is operated correctly.

6. The leaders take an inventory of the total assets acquired during the year and then carefully examine the capabilities of the various stewards to see where these new assets can be profitably assigned. If it has been a particularly good year, they may even decide to declare a dividend and give each family an equal share. Each family then will use the money for whatever purpose it desires.

Both the dividend and the increase in one's stewardship become the steward's legal property.

Some groups who have experimented with this program have tried to do it on the basis of a commune, but this is fatal. A modern commune works no better today than did those set up at Jamestown and Plymouth 350 years ago.

7. The size of the group is important. To make these communities work successfully, they must be large enough to share the risk and absorb the impact of sickness, accidents, fire, crop failure, old age, and disease. In a highly integrated covenant society, these risks are assumed by the entire community. Therefore, whenever any of these afflictions occur, the whole body of the people unite to remedy the situation. Thus, to guard against some overwhelming calamity or injury to a large number, the community or group of communities must be of sufficient size to "share the risk and absorb the impact" of whatever happens.

8. Where major industrial development or community service projects are involved, it may be advisable for several covenant communities to unite together. This would be true of hospitals, manufacturing, institutions of higher learning, making mass purchases, providing inter-community transportation, building roads, and so forth.

9. As we have previously indicated, God's law requires that the community be organized in God's way.

In order to deploy responsibilities as well as to receive benefits, it is important to divide the families of the community into groups of ten (with each group electing a leader), then unite five of these groups to comprise fifty families (who elect a leader), then two groups of fifty are united to comprise a hundred (who elect a leader), then ten of these "hundreds" unite to make a thousand families (who elect a leader), and so forth. This is a highly democratic system where all adults have a voice and a vote in electing their leaders from the captains of ten right on up to the highest level of government.

10. This graduated hierarchy of community structure is extremely important insofar as the administration of justice is concerned. The decision of any judge can be appealed to the higher judges from level to level until the individual feels he or she has received a full measure of justice. The line of appeal can go clear up to the presiding council.

11. The judges must be thoroughly trained in every aspect of the law. Since the parties to a dispute are not represented by lawyers, the judges must do the interrogating and—where necessary—conduct a thorough investigation on their own. The purpose of the hearing is to attain the highest possible level of fairness and justice for all concerned. It is also extremely important that the judges continually send out the message that the law will be strictly enforced and that crime does not pay. As we have already seen, the structure of God's law is set up by design to emphasize to all mischief-minded individuals that the penalties for misconduct are intended to be a positive deterrent.

12. The very nature of a stewardship community is to promote prosperity, peace, and freedom for its people. The success of such a society is enhanced by a vigorous proselyting and training program to attract those on the outside so they can qualify for membership. The ultimate goal is to have the whole population thriving and prospering within the ranks of this vast network of stewardship communities.

WHAT ABOUT THOSE WHO ARE NOT UNDER THE STEWARDSHIP PRINCIPLE?

Even before the Founders knew how to set up a perfect Zion society as visualized by John Adams and Thomas Jefferson, the Founders knew how to provide a constitutional structure which would be conducive to peace, happiness, and prosperity IF THE POLITICIANS DIDN'T CHANGE IT.

Just for comparison purposes, let us remind ourselves what it would have been like if the United States had retained the inspired formula of the original Constitution.

1. There would be no income taxes, no returns, and no audits.

2. There would be no withholding tax.

3. There would be no federal social security taxes, since the advantages of private social security would make the federal program obsolete.

4. Taxes would be as the Founders intended—based on an excise or sales tax, where the rich pay more because they buy more.

5. There would be no national debt.

6. There would be no deficit spending.

7. The notorious Butler case of 1936 would never have been allowed. This is the decision of the Supreme Court which unlawfully changed the "general" welfare clause to include "private" welfare. This opened the floodgates to socialism, profligate spending, and boosted the budget from 6 billion in 1936 to 600 billion by 1980, and to over a trillion by 1990. By 2010, that number has reached 3.6 trillion—that's 3.6 million millions.

8. There would be an honest money system based on gold and silver as the Constitution originally intended. All currency would be redeemable in gold or silver on demand.

9. The Federal Reserve would have been ruled unconstitutional. Even today, the Federal Reserve can be repealed by a majority of Congress under paragraph 31 of its charter and have all its assets turned over to the U.S. Treasury as required by the original act.

10. No bank would be allowed to advance credit based on taxpayers' bonds, or to create fiat money, meaning create paper money out of nothing or without anything of value to back it.

11. Charter banks by the federal government, as well as the states,

would have to make loans on existing assets, just as the government requires in Singapore today. The Singapore banks are flourishing because the people trust them.

12. Profits from the U.S. National Bank would go into the nation's general fund to cut down taxes.

13. Profits from the state banks would go to the states to cut down state taxes.

14. No further foreign aid, would be permitted since there is no authority for foreign aid in the Constitution.

15. Under God's system of judges, poverty and crime would be virtually eliminated. The need for prisons would be minimal.

16. Justice would be administered on the basic principle of reparation to the victim instead of fines going to the state or federal government. Jefferson emphasized how well this principle worked for the Anglo-Saxons as well as ancient Israel.

17. There would be no Federal Education Agency which the Founders warned against, most vehemently.

18. There would be no federal Medicare and Medicaid system, nor would there be national health care services. All of these services would be supplied by the local community or county. The government's expensive and inefficient boondoggle promised so much to everybody that soon the entire health care system was in jeopardy. The younger generation has forgotten that before the government got its tentacles into the system, hospitals were cheaper and more efficient while being run by the Catholics, Seventh-day Adventists, Methodists, Baptists, Shriners, and Latter-day Saints. The county hospitals could afford to take practically anyone because the doctors all volunteered to work on the needy a certain percentage of the time, free of charge.

19. All federal agencies would be subject to a sunset law—if they could not pass muster on constitutional grounds, they would be terminated at the end of the next fiscal year.

20. There probably would be no 14th Amendment (which allows federal courts to intervene in state criminal cases). Certainly there would be no 16th Amendment (which gave Congress power to extract income tax), no 17th Amendment (with senators becoming popularly elected instead of appointed, thus losing their role of guarding state rights and sovereignty), no 23rd Amendment (which gives residents in the seat of government, Washington D.C., the power to vote), and the 25th Amendment would be sharply revised (giving the president power freely to appoint a successor for vice president, without having Congress conduct a more scrutinized approval process with a two-thirds vote).

BOTH GOD'S LAW AND A ZION SOCIETY ARE IN AMERICA'S FUTURE

Although, as we have said, it may take some remarkable circumstances to bring it about, there is a point on God's time line when America will fulfill a remarkable role. Daniel saw it, and so did Moses. Isaiah saw it, and so did Malachi.

Meanwhile, all of us have certain immediate tasks:

1. We should take every precaution, as well as positive steps, to stabilize our families.

2. We should practice frugality and sacrifice, where necessary, to get completely out of debt.

3. We should have an adequate storage supply of food, fuel, and warm clothes that will last at least a year.

4. We should carefully study God's law so we can explain its advantages when people are frightened and need hope and encouragement.

5. We should stay close to the Author of God's law. Read the scriptures every day.

6. Lastly, we should keep our eyes on God's time line and never forget that Moses said:

"And it shall come to pass, when all these things are come upon thee [the Israelites], the blessing and the curse, which I have set before thee, and thou shalt call them to mind among all the nations, whither the LORD thy God hath driven thee. . . .

"And thou shalt return and obey the voice of the LORD, and do all his commandments which I command thee this day.

"And the LORD thy God will make thee plenteous in every work of thine hand, in the fruit of thy body, and in the fruit of thy cattle, and in the fruit of thy land, for good: for the LORD will again rejoice over thee for good, as he rejoiced over thy fathers." [13]

* * * *

TOPICS FOR REFLECTION AND DISCUSSION

1. Who wrote a book in the days of the Founding Fathers which outlined the principles for an ideal free enterprise system of economics? What kind of freedom was it designed to preserve?

2. Among a virtuous people, what is the special rule that makes their economy work smoothly and fairly? Can you think of one good reason to have the money system based on gold and silver? If the people want paper currency for convenience, what must they be able to get for their paper currency "on demand"?

3. Who ran for president of the United States and recommended a banking system administered by the national government? What would the profits be used for? What would the state branches of the national bank do with their profits? Could there still be private banks? Would they be insured by the government?

4. Under God's law, would there still be insurance companies? Describe three things that would be different for the profession of practicing law under God's law.

5. Explain what it means to have the jury determine both the "law and the facts." Why did the Founders feel this was a safety net to protect the freedom and rights of the people?

6. Explain how the health care system would work under God's law. Explain who would be responsible for the education of the children. What five religious principles would be taught in the schools? Would there be separate schools for the poor?

7. What is the greatest curse of modern cities? About how many people would live in a community under God's law? How much acreage would surround the town for farming and stock?

8. Out of the eight advantages of a Zion society, can you name three? Can anybody be required to enter a Zion society? Does his stewardship belong to him, or does he just operate it as a type of share cropper? If he is a farmer, how much does he get to keep when the crop is harvested? What happens to all the rest?

9. Since there will be some who are not in the Zion society, list four advantages they nevertheless will have by living under the free enterprise system of the restored Constitution.

10. List three heavy burdens which Americans carry now that they would not have to endure after God's law has been adopted under the restored Constitution.

1. *Journal of Discourses*, vol. 10, p. 356.
2. Ibid.
3. *History of the Church*, vol. vi, p. 206
4. Will Durant, *The Age of Louis XIV*, New York: Simon and Schuster, 1963, p. 184
5. Skousen, *The Making of America*, op. cit., pp. 615-17
6. Ibid.
7. *History of the Church*, vol 1. p. 358, emphasis added
8. Moses 7:68
9. 4 Nephi, verses 15-22
10. Acts 4:32-25
11. Alma 1:26-31; Mosiah 4:14-16
12. D&C 82:17
13. Deuteronomy 30:1-9

CHAPTER SIX

THE LAW OF CONSECRATION

In the previous chapter, we covered the dual system of economics that will prevail after the cleansing of America when there will be a restoration of the Constitution and the setting up of God's law.

In this present chapter, we will cover in much greater detail the law of consecration that we briefly mentioned earlier. The following presentation was prepared while this author was teaching at Brigham Young University, and it is included in this chapter to make certain that all of the significant aspects of this divine system have been covered.

INTRODUCTION

One of the most fascinating subjects to be studied and understood by the Saints is the Lord's law of consecration. Since those who have gone through the temple are committed to live this law WHEN CALLED UPON, it is an appropriate subject for careful study. In fact, many of its principles can be applied in the daily lives of the Saints, pending the time when the fullness of the law of consecration will be established under the direction of the First Presidency.

THE SPIRITUAL ENVIRONMENT
REQUIRED FOR THIS LAW

Enoch established the first "City of Zion" under the law of consecration around 2,483 B.C., when Enoch was apparently sixty-five years of age. [1] During a period of 365 years, he was able to refine his people until it says, "the Lord came and dwelt with his people." [2] The scripture also says "there was no poor among them," [3] and eventually they were all translated. [4]

In a modern revelation, the Lord said,

"Enoch and his brethren . . . were separated from the earth and were received unto myself—a city reserved until a day of righteousness shall come." [5]

Joseph Smith said:

"Their place of habitation is that of the terrestrial order, and a place prepared for such characters [whom] He held in reserve to be ministering angels unto many planets, and who as yet have not entered into so great a fullness as those who are resurrected from the dead." [6]

Probably the most comprehensive description of the spiritual climate which Enoch and other Zion societies were able to create is captured in the words of Orson Pratt. He said:

"One of the most beautiful characteristics of the ante-diluvian Zion, was that 'they were of one heart and one mind, and there were no poor among them,' a perfect union of sentiment and feeling: no bitterness—no hatred—no slandering or reviling—no defrauding or taking advantage one of another—no person seeking to aggrandize himself by heaping up riches while others were poor—no selfishness or pride—no hypocrisy or affectation: but every one loved his neighbor as himself—every man studied the welfare of the whole—every one considered himself as only a steward over the things committed to his charge; it was all considered the Lord's, and ready to appropriate for any purpose which the Lord should direct.

"They were equal in earthly things, therefore the Lord made them equal in heavenly things. Nothing short of continued revelation could ever have brought about an order of things so perfect.

"Such union was strength and power; such oneness was after the order of heaven; the powers of the earth could not hold them—the laws of nature could not retain them; their faith laid hold on immortality—on eternal life—on the powers of heaven—on heavenly things; the veil was parted and could no more be closed—the city of Zion fled from earth to heaven there to be reserved until a day of righteousness should come when the earth should rest. . . ." [7]

A similar spiritual climate was developed by Melchizedek during the days of Abraham. His great city was called Salem (where authorities think Jerusalem is today).

Concerning him, the scripture says:

"But Melchizedek, having . . . received the office of the high priesthood . . . did preach repentance unto his people. And behold, they did repent; and Melchizedek did establish peace in the land in his days; therefore he was called the prince of peace. . . ." [8]

A modern revelation says:

"And now, Melchizedek was a priest of this order; therefore he obtained peace in Salem, and was called the prince of peace. And his people wrought righteousness and obtained heaven, and sought for the city of Enoch which God had before taken, separating it from the earth, having reserved it unto the latter days or the end of the world." [9]

The same type of society was established during the golden age of the Nephites:

"And it came to pass in the thirty and sixth year, the people were all converted unto the Lord, upon all the face of the land, both Nephites and Lamanites, and there were no contentions and disputations among them, and every man did deal justly one with another. And they had all things common among them; therefore there were not rich and poor, bond and free, but they were all made free, and partakers of the heavenly gift." [10]

It also says:

"And there were no envyings, nor strifes, nor tumults, nor whoredoms, nor lyings, nor murders, nor any manner of lasciviousness; and surely there could not be a happier people among all the people who had been created by the hand of God." [11]

During the ministry of the apostles in Palestine, an attempt was made to carry out these same principles. The scripture says:

"And the multitude of them that believed were of one heart and of one soul: neither said any of them that ought [any] of the things which he possessed was his own; but they had ALL THINGS COMMON . . . Neither was there any among them that lacked: for as many as were possessors of lands or houses sold them, and brought the prices of the things that were sold, and laid them down at the apostles' feet: and distribution was made unto every man according as he had need." [12]

These few verses led many to assume that the early Christians practiced communism—that they gave up all their private property and put it in a common pool to be administered by the apostles. However, now that the Lord has revealed the nature of the law of consecration in modern times, we have a better understanding of what really happened.

Each man or each couple entered a covenant to treat his property as a STEWARDSHIP UNDER GOD. They retained legal title to the property but SAID that it was not their own. It was God's, and must therefore be used for the benefit of all the Saints. In order for everyone to have some kind of stewardship, it was necessary for those who had a surplus to VOLUNTARILY decide what they would sell or donate so the proceeds could be given to the apostles for distribution to the poor, and thereby give the poor some means of making a living.

HOW THE APOSTLES HANDLED THE LAW OF CONSECRATION

That this was the procedure in the days of the Apostles can be demonstrated in the very next chapter of Acts. There we find two of the members of the Church (Ananias and his wife, Sapphira) voluntarily deciding to sell part of their covenant stewardship property and give the money to the apostles.

But they decided to keep back part of the price and tell the apostles that the smaller amount was all they were able to get for the field. The Spirit whispered to Peter what they had done, and this led Peter to severely reprimand them. At the same time, he pointed out the true nature of property rights under the stewardship principle and said:

"Why hath Satan filled thine heart to lie to the Holy Ghost, and to keep back part of the price of the land? Whilst it [the land] remained, WAS NOT IT THINE OWN? and after it was sold, was not it [the money] IN THINE OWN POWER? Why hast thou conceived this thing in thine heart? Thou hast not lied unto men, but unto God" (showing that the property was already under a stewardship covenant). [13]

Commenting on this passage, Dummelow's Bible Commentary says:

"The Church of Jerusalem recognized the principle of private property. A disciple's property really was his own, but he did not say it was his own; he treated it as if it were common property."

This entire circumstance demonstrates the absolute necessity of developing a rich SPIRITUAL CLIMATE before the law of consecration can operate as it should.

How To Build The Spiritual Climate For The Law Of Consecration

The modern leaders of the Church have already emphasized that the Church is gradually being prepared for the day when some of the Saints will be called forth to initiate the law of consecration. They have even outlined in the Church Welfare manual the basic principles which must exist in order to have the spiritual climate needed for the Law of Consecration.

First of all, a person desiring to live under the law of consecration must demonstrate in his personal life that he is not a "transgressor" of God's commandments, but obeys the word of God "with strictness." Here is the way the Lord said it:

"For I, the Lord, have decreed in my heart, that inasmuch as any man belonging to the order [of consecration] shall be found a transgressor, or, in other words, shall break the covenant with which ye are bound, he shall be cursed in his life, and shall be trodden down by whom I will; for I, the Lord, am not to be mocked in these things. . . .

"And I now give unto you power from this very hour, that if any man among you, of the order, is found a TRANSGRESSOR, and repenteth not of the evil, that ye shall deliver him over unto the buffetings of Satan; and he shall not have power to bring evil upon you." [14]

This was a command to constantly cleanse the society of the Saints of those who were transgressors. Otherwise, they would corrupt the society and "bring evil upon you."

Next, the saints were to be trained to think of "property" as a "stewardship under God." The earth belongs to the Lord and we are merely "custodians" of earthly possessions during our mortal lives. The Lord says:

"For it is expedient that I, the Lord, should make every man accountable, as a steward over earthly blessings, which I have made and prepared for my creatures. I, the Lord, stretched out the heavens, and built the earth, my very handiwork; AND ALL THINGS THEREIN ARE MINE. And it is my purpose to provide for my saints, for ALL THINGS ARE MINE." [15]

Third, the fatherhood of God and the brotherhood of man require that human beings look upon one another as members of the same family—the family of God, and they are directly responsible for one another's welfare. The Lord says:

"Therefore, if any man shall take of the abundance made, and impart not his portion, according to the law of my gospel, unto the poor and the needy, he shall, with the wicked, lift up his eyes in hell, being in torment." [16]

Fourth, the Lord assures us that there is no need for us to worry about over-population:

"For the earth is full [of resources], and there is enough and to spare." [17]

The reason huge nations usually find it difficult to feed themselves is because of two factors: (1) failure to maintain the necessary level of individual productivity, and (2) allowing monopolies to develop so that the people become divided into the extremely rich and the extremely poor. Where these conditions exist, there will be starvation even among SMALL populations.

The Lord's solution to the first problem is to place on each man and woman a MORAL responsibility to work—to do his share, and to provide for himself and his dependents. He says,

"Thou shalt not be idle; for he that is idle SHALL NOT EAT THE BREAD NOR WEAR THE GARMENTS OF THE LABORER." [18]

In another place, the Lord says:

"Wo unto you poor men, whose hearts are not broken, whose spirits are not contrite, and whose bellies are not satisfied, and whose hands are not stayed from laying hold upon other men's goods, whose eyes are full of greediness, and who WILL NOT LABOR WITH YOUR OWN HANDS!" [19]

He says:

"Thou shalt not IDLE AWAY THY TIME, neither shalt thou BURY THY TALENT that it may not be known." [20]

He even says,

"And the idler SHALL NOT HAVE PLACE IN THE CHURCH, except he repent and mend his ways." [21]

The Lord's solution to the second problem—the monopoly of wealth and resources in a few hands—is voluntary generosity on the part of the rich, whereby all may gain a stewardship and the means of making an honorable living. He says:

"And it is my purpose to provide for my saints, for all things are mine. But it must be done in MINE OWN WAY; and behold THIS is the way that I, the Lord, have decreed to provide for my Saints, THAT THE POOR SHALL BE EXALTED, IN THAT THE RICH ARE MADE LOW." [22]

The rich are made low by converting them to the gospel and teaching them to share in the good things of the earth. If they will not, they stand condemned before God, who declared:

"Wo unto you rich men, that will not give your substance to the poor, for your riches will canker your souls; and this shall be your lamentation in the day of visitation, and of Judgment, and of indignation: The harvest is past, the summer is ended, and my soul is not saved!" [23]

In other words, a rich member of the Church who is not willing to help exalt the poor AUTOMATICALLY LOSES HIS SALVATION!

However, we are not to assume from this that there is an absolute leveling of wealth under the law of consecration. Strange as it would seem, this would destroy the "equality" of the members. The way that men become "equal" under the law of consecration is far-more gratifying and self-fulfilling than merely "sharing the wealth."

This will become apparent as we discuss the operational mechanics of the stewardship system under the law of consecration.

How The Law Of Consecration Worked

Joseph Smith learned about the Lord's law of consecration and stewardship as a result of his experience with a branch of the Church at Kirtland, Ohio.

When he arrived there in January, 1832, Joseph Smith found the branch organized into a commune where they had "common stock" and lived together as "the family." It was immediately apparent to the young prophet that "some strange notions and false spirits had crept in among them." [24] He therefore inquired of the Lord and learned that the Saints should no longer practice their communal stock system, but "receive MY law." [25] Joseph Smith recorded that he had no difficulty getting the new converts to "readily" abandon what they had been doing. [26]

The Lord first commanded that a bishop should be ordained. He named Edward Partridge for this assignment. [27]

Five days later, on February 9, 1832, the Lord set forth the initial framework for the law of consecration and stewardship. This is in Doctrine and Covenants, Section 42. Additional details were given in other revelations as they were needed.

1. First of all, the Saints must make up their minds to love the Lord and keep all His commandments. [28]

2. Then they must "consecrate" their properties to the Lord "with a covenant and a deed which cannot be broken." [29]

3. These properties are then to be placed in the hands of the bishop and his counselors for distribution. [30]

4. Each "steward" or member then receives his "portion." This must be "sufficient for himself and family." [31] This is accomplished by having the bishop distribute the stewardships in such a way that EACH member would be "EQUAL according to his FAMILY, according to his CIRCUMSTANCES, and his WANTS and NEEDS." [32] But only if his wants and needs are "just" will they be granted. [33]

5. Whatever stewardship property a man receives must be "deeded unto him" and "made sure, according to the laws of the land." It remains his, even if he leaves the order! [34]

However, since it is "consecrated" property, the steward will be required of God to "render an account of his stewardship" over that property—"both in time and eternity." [35] Under the laws of the land, "private property" is deeded to the steward by the bishop, but under God's law, the matter goes much further. It is consecrated property for which the Lord will require an accounting, even if the steward takes it out of the order. The same rule applies if a person is excommunicated. As the Lord says:

"And if they are not faithful they shall not have fellowship in the Church; yet they may remain upon their inheritances according to the laws of the land." [36]

6. If he receives back less than he gave, the residue is to remain the property of the Church for distribution to others in need. [37] This surplus residue can never be claimed by the donor once it is deeded over to the Church. [38]

7. Thereafter, ". . . every man shall be made accountable unto me, a steward over his own property." [39] He transacts all business in connection with his stewardship in his own name. [40] He is to treat his stewardship as a "talent" which is to be developed and improved until he "may gain other talents, yea even an hundred fold." [41]

The better he becomes in managing his affairs, and the more productive his stewardship becomes, the more he is able to "cast into the Lord's storehouse, to become the common property of the whole church—every man seeking the interest of his neighbor, and doing all things with an eye single to the glory of God." [42]

8. All the stewards are to have "equal claims on the properties [being held in common], for the benefit of managing the concerns of your stewardships, every man according to his wants and his needs, inasmuch as his wants are just." [43]

9. The common storehouse and common treasury also are set up to provide work and assistance for the poor and needy, [44] to care for the widows and orphans, [45] to pay the bishop and other full-time administrators in the order, [46] to buy new land, to build churches, and eventually to build up the New Jerusalem, [47] to provide operating funds for stewardships, and to provide funds for improving stewardships. [48]

10. Parents may use their stewardship to develop additional stewardships for their maturing children. If they are unable to do so, or the children desire a different type of stewardship, it is provided by the bishop from the treasury and common storehouse. [49]

TITHING

It will be clear from the above that the mission of the steward is to provide for the needs and justifiable "wants" of his family and then turn all the surplus over to the bishop for the central storehouse. [50] However, if a person had no surplus over and above the needs of his family, then he would pay a tithe on all the increment that he and his family had enjoyed during the year. [51] In other words, every steward would make a contribution, the very minimum being a tithe.

This also would be true of a steward who had an assignment of service such as a teacher, administrator, etc., where the quality of service could continually be improved and multiplied but there would be no monetary "increase" to contribute. The contribution of stewards in this category would be a tithe of whatever compensation they had received.

THE RIGHTS OF EACH STEWARD

Respect for the dignity and free agency of each steward is inherent in the system. The system gives the individual all of the following: [52]

1. The right to a stewardship sufficient to care for the needs and wants of himself and his family.

2. The right to negotiate with the bishop and high council for the size and kind of stewardship he desires, as well as improvements thereon.

3. The right to own his stewardship outright, and have a deed to prove it.

4. The right to manage his stewardship as he wishes. The bishop and others may make suggestions, but the steward has the final determination.

5. The right to vote on major expenditures from the community fund.

6. The right, along with every other steward, to draw funds from the treasury to expand and develop his stewardship.

7. The right to receive help from the storehouse in the "event of reverses."

8. The right to have his widow and orphans supported from the storehouse in case he dies.

9. The right to receive medical care and support of his family in case of illness or an accident.

10. The right to have his children receive stewardships when they come of age.

11. The right to leave the system at any time and keep his stewardship as private property.

COOPERATIVE ENTERPRISES

It is understood, of course, that each Zion community under the law of consecration and stewardship will be independent and self-sufficient to the greatest possible extent. However, in a complex society, there are some projects which are too large for a single community to undertake. Or there needs to be an exchange of goods between the various Zion communities in order to take advantage of those things in which each community specializes.

This coordination of cooperative enterprises will be under the supervision of the leading executives of the Order and will be called the "United Order," or the "United Firm." As we shall see later, the term, United Order, was used by the Utah pioneers for cooperative communal projects such as "Orderville." But these were doomed to failure and should have been called by some other name.

HOW DOES ONE GAIN ADMISSION TO A ZION SOCIETY?

As one would expect, high standards are required of those who desire to enter a Zion society.

The first task is to demonstrate over a substantial period of time that one is willing to obey the commandments of God "with strictness."

It must also be evident that a person has overcome the primary instincts of human nature. Some of the most difficult instincts of human nature are GREED, or the passion for the acquisition of "things;" JEALOUSY, which arises when the bishop grants more to one steward than another (just as Jesus did in the parable of the pounds and the parable of the talents); and PRIDE, when one is asked to fill an assignment or role more humble than the one for which the steward aspires or may feel more capable of filling a stewardship to which someone else has been assigned.

Excellent training in the Church for the development of these qualities of humility, suppressing jealousy, and accepting assignments where needed is demonstrated continually. Recently, our stake president was released and asked to teach a class of little girls in Sunday School, and he loved it. He said it was the best job he ever had. We see general authorities at a certain age given emeritus status after serving in some of the highest positions in the Church.

THE ADMISSION PROCEDURE

As we have already indicated, when a person feels ready to enter the Order, he goes to the bishop and expresses a desire to be considered for membership. If approved, he then prepares deeds or contracts by which he will transfer all his property over to the bishop.

After discussing his circumstances and his needs, the bishop then deeds back to him whatever he will need for his new stewardship. If a steward's donation was not enough, he will be given more than he contributed in order to get him started in his new stewardship assignment. If there is more than enough, the "surplus" will be retained by the bishop to assist the poor or help strengthen other stewardships.

During this negotiation to determine the extent of the new stewardship, there might be a misunderstanding. Therefore Joseph Smith wrote:

"The matter of consecration must be done by the mutual consent of both parties; for to give the Bishop power to say how much every man shall have, and he be compelled to comply with the Bishop's judgment is giving the Bishop more power than a king has; and, upon the other hand, to let every man say how much he needs, and the Bishop be compelled to comply with his judgment is to throw Zion into confusion and make a slave of the Bishop. The fact is, there must be a balance or equilibrium of power between the Bishop and the people; and thus harmony and good will may be preserved among you.

"Therefore, those persons consecrating property to the Bishop in Zion, and then receiving an inheritance back, must reasonably show to the Bishop that they need as much as they claim. But in case the two parties cannot come to a mutual agreement, the Bishop is to have nothing to do about receiving such consecrations; and the case must be laid before a council of twelve High Priests. . . ." [53]

Some have thought that the law of consecration was restricted to an agrarian or farm society. Actually, it is designed to fit the most advanced technological cultures. Men who are needed as workers can have their jobs assigned to them as their stewardship and receive a regular wage. This would not only apply to industrial workers, but to teachers, clerks, farmhands, secretaries, equipment operators, service attendants, and a multitude of similar occupations. In due time, a worker (such as a farmhand) could apply for a stewardship of his own.

THE HISTORY OF EARLY EXPERIMENTS WITH THE LAW OF CONSECRATION

The first attempts to establish the law of consecration and stewardship was at Thompson, Ohio, in May, 1831. The participants were Saints from Coleville, New York, who had immigrated to Ohio and had settled at Thompson, which was not far from Kirtland. This program did not get completely organized before the Lord instructed them to go to Missouri, where the center stake of Zion was going to be built. [54]

The second attempt to institute the law of consecration was in Jackson County, Missouri. The inability of the Saints to establish an adequate spiritual discipline, combined with an overflowing influx of a great many poor, led to confusion and eventual persecution. In due time, the Saints were driven completely out of Missouri under the extermination order of Governor Boggs. It will be seen, therefore, that the system was never properly developed or thoroughly tested in Missouri. [55]

When the Saints were driven to Illinois, there were some who settled in Montrose, Iowa, across the river from Nauvoo. These people tried to initiate the law of consecration once more, but when Joseph Smith escaped from his captors in Missouri and joined the Saints at Nauvoo, he soon became aware of what the Saints were doing in Montrose. Joseph crossed the river and said to them:

"The law of consecration could not be kept here, and that it was the will of the Lord that we should desist from trying to keep it; and if persisted in, it would produce a perfect defeat of its object, and that he assumed the whole responsibility of not keeping it until proposed by himself." [56]

This was in accordance with an earlier revelation in which the Lord had said:

"And let those commandments which I have given concerning Zion and her law be executed and fulfilled, AFTER HER REDEMPTION." [57]

Many have supposed that an attempt was made to practice the law of consecration and stewardship in Utah, but such was not the case. It was a completely different approach designed as a temporary program to meet emergency conditions and economic stress:

"It will be observed that Joseph Smith always referred to his new social order as 'The Law of Consecration and Stewardship,' whereas the Utah experiments established under the direction of Brigham Young were called the 'United Order'. . . .

"The United Order, as it was established in Utah, was a modification of the stewardship plans instituted in Ohio and Missouri. Those who participated in the Utah movement consecrated all of their property to the United Order Corporation, but lived as one big family, and NOT AS STEWARDSHIPS INDIVIDUALLY OPERATED. The consecrated property was community property and was managed by the chosen leaders of the Order.

"The members of the Order were assigned to different tasks and types of work by the leaders, according to the program of work outlined from day to day.

"In Orderville, where the plan was operated more idealistically, the families all ate at one table, lived in 'shanties,' all grouped together, and worked as a unit in all enterprises—'all for one and one for all.' There were no individual holdings, no individual management, and no family operated units. . . .

"The United Order was officially brought to an end in 1882 by President Taylor. . . ." [58]

How Can We Best Prepare Ourselves For The Law Of The Lord Which Is Coming?

The Lord has instituted three major programs to prepare the Saints for life in a Zion community.

TITHING. This principle requires that one tenth of all the interest or increase which has come to a person each year be paid into the tithing funds of the Church to do the Lord's work. It not only provides the primary means for financing the entire Church, but also serves as a yardstick to measure the loyalty of Church members. As President Joseph F. Smith said:

"By this principle it shall be known who is for the kingdom of God and who is against it. By this principle it shall be seen whose hearts are set on doing the will of God and keeping His commandments, thereby sanctifying the land of Zion unto God, and who are opposed to this principle and HAVE CUT THEMSELVES OFF FROM THE BLESSINGS OF ZION." [59]

The importance which the Lord attaches to this principle is reflected in a modern revelation, which says:

"Behold, now it is called today until the coming of the Son of Man, and verily it is a day of sacrifice, and a day for the tithing of my people; FOR HE THAT IS TITHED SHALL NOT BE BURNED AT HIS COMING." [60]

FAST OFFERINGS. This is not a modern institution, but has been used by the Lord in ages past. The Lord referred to it in the days of Isaiah:

"Is not this the fast that I have chosen? . . . Is it not to DEAL THY BREAD TO THE HUNGRY, and that thou bring the poor that are cast out to thy house? when thou seest the naked, that thou cover him; and that thou hide not thyself from thine own flesh?" [61]

So one of the chief purposes of "organized fasting" by the Church is to gather together the equivalent of the food which was not eaten and make it available to the poor. But this is the very minimum requirement, to donate the cost of the meals not eaten. The fast offering is the means by which organized care for the poor is handled, and surely those who have means cannot be saved without being generous to the poor. [62]

We should give liberal donations to the Fast Offering Fund over and above the cost of the meals not eaten. Alma told the Saints of his day to:

"Impart of their substance, every one according to that which he had; if he have MORE ABUNDANTLY, he should IMPART more abundantly; and of him that had but little, but little should be required; and to him that had not should be given. And thus they should impart of their own free will and good desires towards God. . . ." [63]

CHURCH WELFARE PROGRAM

King Benjamin said that in caring for the poor,

"See that all these things are done in WISDOM AND ORDER; for it is not requisite that a man should run faster than he has strength." [64]

When the Great Depression hit the United States during the 1930s, it was found that tithing and fast offerings were not adequate to care for the poor in such an emergency. The Church was soon running beyond its strength and the need for more "wisdom and order" became vividly apparent. There was no program in the Church where the unemployed could go to help "earn their keep." Instead, the bishops were giving "handouts." It was revealed to the president of the Church that this must stop and a program developed wherein the poor could be assisted in helping themselves. As the Lord had said a century earlier,

"And it is my purpose that my saints be provided for . . . but it must needs be done in mine own way." [65]

By 1936, the First Presidency had worked out the basic structure for such a program.

It was to be a "system under which the curse of idleness would be done away with, the evils of a dole abolished, and independence, thrift and self-respect be once more established amongst our people." [66]

In this same statement, the First Presidency said,

"The aim of the Church is to help the people to help themselves. Work is to be re-enthroned as the ruling principle of the lives of our Church membership."

The Church thereupon undertook a long-range program to teach the Saints that the primary responsibility for temporal well-being rests upon the individual, then upon his relatives, and finally, upon the body of the Church.

SUGGESTIONS FROM THE FIRST PRESIDENCY

To be protected from the trauma of depression or disaster, each family was urged to:

1. Get out of debt.

2. Have a home free of any mortgage, if possible.

3. Live within the income.

4. Consistently save a little.

5. Have on hand at least a year's supply of food, clothing, fuel and funds.

6. Commence learning how to be self-sustaining by planting gardens, storing dehydrates as well as perishables, making bedding and clothes, practicing thrift, and living frugally.

7. Be prepared to share with the less fortunate, but use "wisdom and order" so as not to run beyond one's strength.

WELFARE PROJECTS

The Church commenced setting up welfare projects wherever there was a sufficient number of Saints to justify it. These included farms, cattle ranches, fruit orchards, flour mills, shoe factories, textile mills, canneries, repair shops, mattress factories, etc.

The Church also set up the Deseret Industries, where people could donate their surplus clothes, furniture, and appliances, and deserving unemployed could have the opportunity of cleaning and repairing these items for re-sale.

Although a deep depression could still cause very serious dislocation among many members of the Church, the fact remains that the general membership is in a much stronger position to protect itself from disaster than ever before. What is even more important, the Saints are learning HOW to create a society in which the law of consecration and stewardship can be adopted AT A LATER TIME. As Joseph Smith indicated, it is extremely important to make no attempt to set up the law of consecration or a Zion society until it has been authorized by the Lord.

* * * *

TOPICS FOR REFLECTION AND DISCUSSION

1. According to the scriptures, when was the law of consecration practiced on a large scale for the first time? Who set it up? Who told him how to do it? Can you name three other people who practiced these same principles?

2. Why do you think the Lord was so strict in rooting out "transgressors" who refused to repent? How did the Lord want His people to look upon their property? How did the Lord want us to look upon our fellow men?

3. What are the two major reasons why huge nations often find it difficult to feed themselves? What does the Lord say about work? What does He say about laziness? Can prolonged and deliberate idleness jeopardize a person's membership in the Church?

4. Who among the rich does the Lord condemn? Who among the poor does the Lord condemn? When a person receives an inheritance of consecrated property, how long does the consecration last? What happens if that person takes that property out of the Order? What happens if he is excommunicated from the Church?

5. Can you name five "rights" of a steward under the law of consecration? Would there be large corporations or cooperative enterprises under the law of consecration?

6. Can you trace the process which a person would follow in gaining admission to a Zion society and the law of consecration? What if there is a disagreement between the bishop and the steward over the arrangement? Did Joseph Smith anticipate this?

7. What elements of human nature are most likely to prevent a person from entering a Zion society? Name three things the Church is doing to prepare its people for the law of consecration.

8. Why did the law of consecration fail in Missouri? What did Joseph Smith tell the Saints in Montrose when they tried to practice it again? Does this still apply today?

9. Was the Utah "United Order" the law of consecration? Had this same setup failed in Jamestown? How about Plymouth? What has the Lord instituted in the Church to help the Saints prepare for any catastrophe or economic collapse?

10. Can you name five of the suggestions coming from the First Presidency to help each family be prepared for any unexpected crisis? On a scale of one to ten, where would you say your family stands in following these suggestions? Have you ever worked on a welfare project? Have you ever volunteered to help out at the Deseret Industries?

---

1. Moses 7:19
2. Moses 7:16
3. Moses 7:18
4. Moses 7:21
5. D&C 45:11-12
6. *Teachings of the Prophet Joseph Smith*, p. 170
7. Parley P. Pratt, *The Seer*, p. 265
8. Alma 13:18-19
9. Inspired Version, Genesis 14:33-34
10. 4 Nephi 1:2-3
11. 4 Nephi l:16
12. Acts 4:32, 34-35
13. Acts 5:3-4
14. D&C 104:5-6; 10
15. D&C 104:13-15
16. D&C 104:18
17. D&C 104:17
18. D&C 42:42
19. D&C 56:17
20. D&C 60:13
21. D&C 75:29

22. D&C 104:15-16
23. D&C 56:16
24. *History of the Church* 1:146
25. D&C 41:3
26. *History of the Church* 1:146-147
27. D&C 41:9-11
28. D&C 42:29
29. D&C 42:30
30. D&C 42:31
31. D&C 42:32
32. D&C 51:3
33. D&C 82:17
34. D&C 51:5-6
35. D&C 72:3
36. D&C 83:3
37. D&C 42:34
38. D&C 42:32
39. D&C 42:32
40. D&C 104:49
41. D&C 82:18
42. D&C 82:18-19
43. D&C 82:17
44. D&C 42:34
45. D&C 83:6
46. D&C 51:14; 72:11
47. D&C 42:35
48. D&C 82:17-18
49. D&C 83:4.-5
50. D&C 42:33-34; 119:1
51. D&C 119:l-3
52. Taken largely from *Liberalism, Conservatism, and Mormonism*, by Hyrum Andrus, pp. 12-14
53. History of the Church 1:364-365
54. *Priesthood and Church Welfare*, Deseret Book, 1938, p. 125
55. Ibid.
56. *History of the Church* 4:93
57. D&C 105:34
58. *Priesthood and Church Welfare*, pp. 126-129

59. *Gospel Doctrine,* 5th ed., pp. 225-226
60. D&C 64:23
61. Isaiah 58:6-8
62. D&C 104:18
63. Mosiah 18:27-28
64. Mosiah 4:27
65. D&C 104:15-16
66. *Conference Report,* October, 1936, p. 37

CHAPTER SEVEN

DEVELOPING GODLY QUALITIES FOR A ZION SOCIETY

One of the most unique qualities of the American Founding Fathers was their profound knowledge of the Bible. Most of them had graduated from colleges or universities designed to prepare men for the ministry. They had therefore studied the scriptures in Latin or Hebrew for the Old Testament and Greek for the New Testament.

At the height of his career, John Adams, second president of the United States, made a remarkable statement which is often quoted. John Adams knew what it would take to set up a Zion society under God's law. He said:

"Suppose a nation in some distant region, should take the BIBLE for their ONLY law book, and every member should regulate his conduct by the precepts there exhibited.

"Every member would be obliged in conscience to temperance and frugality and industry, to justice and kindness and charity towards his fellow men, and to piety and love, and reverence towards almighty God.

"In this commonwealth, no man would impair his health by gluttony, drunkenness, or lust—no man would sacrifice his most precious time to cards, [TV?] or any other trifling and mean amusement—no man would steal or lie or [in] any way defraud his neighbor, but would live in peace and good will with all men—no man would blaspheme his Maker or profane his worship, but a rational and manly, a sincerely and unaffected piety and devotion, would reign in all hearts. . . .

"What a paradise this would be." [1]

Neither a prophet nor an apostle could have said it much better. This is precisely the way God intended the righteous to live in a Zion society.

The principles of a Zion society sometimes are referred to as the Judeo-Christian code. It means living by all the original gospel principles revealed by God to His prophets in the Old Testament, the New Testament and the scriptures revealed in modern times.

In this chapter, we will discuss many of the principal features of godly living which can be practiced even before a Zion society is established. No pattern for happy living ever has been invented which is superior to this one.

WHY WE CAN ONLY ENJOY THE BLESSINGS OF A ZION SOCIETY A MOMENT AT A TIME

As a prelude to reviewing the prospects of a Zion society, we should remind ourselves that during earth life these elements of euphoria and happiness—which we identify with life in a Zion society—can only reign supreme in our thinking and feelings for a few moments at a time. In other words, when circumstances allow us to contemplate the heavenly harmony which we associate with life in Zion, we cannot carve it in stone. It is a fleeting taste of God's future plan of perfect happiness—but a sudden change of circumstances can awaken us from our pleasant reverie and confront us with the horrible shock of the real and the ugly.

When this happens, the challenge is not to continue meditating about Zion, but to act quickly, adjust our attitudes and meet the new challenge in whatever way God has commanded us. It makes us realize that what would be considered a Zion approach to life in dealing with one situation may not at all be appropriate in coping with the real and the ugly when circumstances have suddenly changed.

This was dramatically demonstrated on a Sunday evening, February 7, 1993, when 17,000 young people were gathered in a nineteen-stake fireside at Brigham Young University. They had come to hear Howard W. Hunter, who was then President of the Quorum of the Twelve. One could feel the Spirit of God as this beloved leader rose to address this vast audience while other thousands watched on television at firesides broadcast by satellite all over North America.

As President Hunter stood at the pulpit to begin his address, a voice suddenly rang out, "Stop right there!" A young man carrying a briefcase in one hand and a black object in the other rushed onto the stage. He said he had a bomb and a detonator and ordered everyone to leave the building except President Hunter.

Most of the officials and guests quickly left the stage, and some of those near the exits began hurriedly to rush outside. The man with the briefcase and detonator then handed a letter to President Hunter and told him to read the letter over the microphone [and the satellite network] or he would blow up the building.

What were the feelings of all these godly people at this tremendously critical moment? President Hunter knew enough about insane terrorists to realize that this might be the end of his mortal mission. The two security guards who stood near him knew their lives might also be snuffed out if they stayed at their posts— which they did. Officials and guests who had hurried from the podium knew they were doing what they had been told to do.

President Hunter said quietly and firmly to the terrorist, "I will NOT read that letter."

The whole audience was shocked by what was happening and they knew this whole scenario was terribly wrong. It shouldn't even be happening. Then a few began singing, "We Thank Thee, O God, for a Prophet." Many of the audience stopped where they were and joined in the song. After one verse, they began singing "I Am a Child of God."

While this was going on, a young man approached a few feet from the podium holding a can of Mace in his hand. When he saw the music was distracting the terrorist, he rushed forward and gave the man a heavy dose of demobilizing gas directly into his face. The security officers saw their chance, as did several students nearby. They grabbed the man and wrestled him to the floor. The stunned terrorist immediately was handcuffed and quickly led away.

Everyone returned to their seats and President Hunter took his place at the podium to begin his address by saying: "Life has a fair number of challenges in it." Then he added, "As demonstrated." [2]

The entire audience was impressed tremendously with the calm, matter-of-fact composure of this godly man who could have been killed. Of course, we all have to go sometime, and for President Hunter, perhaps that was it. But the Lord knew this man better than the terrorist. Not many months afterward Howard W. Hunter would be sustained as the new President of the Church of Jesus Christ of Latter-day Saints.

This incident illustrates why we say a Zion quality of life can only be enjoyed a moment at a time. Just when we seem to be enjoying the benign sense of euphoria that we associate with Zion and God's heavenly peace, the whole situation may fractionalize with a thunder clap, and we can find ourselves put to the acid test by circumstances that have nothing to do with Zion or euphoria.

GUIDELINES FOR A ZION SOCIETY

Keeping all this in mind, let us now briefly review some of the major guidelines enunciated by our Heavenly Father for Zion living.

This is a brief inventory of the Lord's scriptures which tell each of us by a spiritual barometer whether our quotient of Zion living is rising or falling.

1. Let us begin with the first and greatest of all God's commandments. In essence it says:

Thou shalt praise and acknowledge the Almighty God who rescued each of us from the abyss of outer darkness and made us part of God's glorious kingdom. [3] Then we are told: You must continually LOVE HIM and look to Him for guidance with all your heart, might, mind and strength. [4]

2. From the beginning, a loving Father has kindly revealed His code of commandments for happy living so we can clearly distinguish between right and wrong. As a consequence, the scripture says: AGAINST NONE IS HIS WRATH KINDLED, SAVE THOSE WHO CONFESS NOT HIS HAND IN ALL THINGS, AND OBEY NOT HIS COMMANDMENTS." [5]

3. Unfortunately, all of us make mistakes and commit sins either large or small. Therefore a loving Heavenly Father has declared: "I command you to REPENT—REPENT, LEST I SMITE YOU BY THE ROD OF MY MOUTH, AND BY MY WRATH, AND BY MY ANGER, AND YOUR SUFFERINGS BE SORE—HOW SORE YOU KNOW NOT, HOW EXQUISITE YOU KNOW NOT, YEA, HOW HARD TO BEAR YOU KNOW NOT." [6]

4. Of course, it isn't hard to say we repent, but that is not enough for the Father. He has provided a sacred ordinance by which we make a total commitment that will remain in effect the rest of our lives. He says: "HE THAT BELIEVETH AND IS BAPTIZED SHALL BE SAVED, BUT HE THAT BELIEVETH NOT SHALL BE DAMNED." [7] So it is by baptism that we promise to serve God and obey His commandments forever.

5. But we human beings are fragile creatures. In order to succeed in life through tribulations and temptations, the Lord has provided

a spiritual guide—a still, small voice of the Holy Spirit or the Holy Ghost—to abide with us so long as we remain worthy.

This, too, is given us through a holy ordinance, and therefore, the Lord says: "And again, it shall come to pass that on as many as ye shall baptize with water, YE SHALL LAY YOUR HANDS, AND THEY SHALL RECEIVE THE GIFT OF THE HOLY GHOST, AND SHALL BE LOOKING FORTH FOR THE SIGNS OF MY COMING." [8] The gift of the Holy Ghost is one of the choicest blessings the Father can give us in this life and it is given to abide with us forever if we cultivate its companionship. This is why the commandment is given as part of the ordinance: "Receive the Holy Ghost!"

6. Once a person has fulfilled the initiatory ordinances of the gospel, the supreme task is to endure to the end. So the scripture reads: "AND, IF YOU KEEP MY COMMANDMENTS AND ENDURE TO THE END YOU SHALL HAVE ETERNAL LIFE, WHICH GIFT IS THE GREATEST OF ALL THE GIFTS OF GOD." [9]

7. But to keep God's commandments requires a specific knowledge of what those commandments are. For example, our Father's children are precious and sacred to Him, therefore He declared, "THOU SHALT NOT KILL." [10] The only exception is when life is taken in self-defense. Otherwise, the taking of human life—with a full knowledge that it is against God's commandment—is next to sinning against the Holy Ghost. When the Lord gave the law to His restored church as it applied to those who had come in under the covenant, He said:

"Thou shalt not kill; and he that kills shall not have forgiveness in this world, NOR IN THE WORLD TO COME." [11]

8. And because private property and personal possessions are the essence of security for life and contribute to human happiness, the mandate of God says THOU SHALT NOT STEAL that which belongs to another, either by fraud or by theft. [12]

9. Another important facet of life is the search for truth. Only by this means can we know whom we can trust and the things upon which we can depend. To deceive another is a serious offense against God, who has said that in all our communications and representations, THOU SHALT NOT LIE nor bear false witness. [13]

10. Because there is a natural tendency to improve one's lot in life by seeking to obtain that which is beautiful or valuable, there is often a temptation to want something which cannot be obtained legitimately. This is a snare for many and therefore God's mandate is: "THOU SHALT NOT COVET THY NEIGHBOR'S GOODS" or try to cheat him out of that which he values most, whether it be his wife or his home. The Lord says, "Thou shalt go out and obtain your own." [14] We call this "the gospel of work." One of the greatest sins of our day is wanting something for nothing. This is COVETING.

11. Parents are blessed to be co-creators with God in producing human beings in God's own image. This is a sacred privilege which God says requires that PARENTS LOVE AND TEACH THEIR CHILDREN. [15] Since children are the offspring of God, it is a great offense against Him when they are neglected, abused, or taught doctrines contrary to the revelations of God.

12. When children come into this world, they are completely helpless, and they remain completely dependent on their parents throughout their early years. This places a responsibility upon the parents to see they are fed, clothed, protected in a comfortable home, and given a sense of being loved and wanted. It is a heinous sin against God when lazy or neglectful parents fail to PROVIDE THESE THINGS FOR THEIR FAMILIES. [16]

13. In order to build the structure of a family according to divine principles, the parents are not the only ones who carry responsibilities. There are reciprocal duties on the part of children to maintain a sacred and respectful attitude toward their parents. Therefore, the Lord says children SHALL HONOR THEIR

FATHER AND THEIR MOTHER THAT THEY MAY HAVE A LONG AND HAPPY LIFE UPON THE EARTH AS GOD DESIGNED THE FAMILY RELATIONSHIP TO PROVIDE. [17]

14. God holds human beings responsible for the way they treat each other, therefore He has declared, THOU SHALT LOVE THY NEIGHBOR AS THYSELF. [18]

15. Or, to put it another way, DO UNTO OTHERS AS YOU WOULD HAVE THEM DO UNTO YOU. [19]

16. Because the power of sexual procreation is a gift of God and very sacred in His sight, God has issued this strict command: "THOU SHALT NOT COMMIT FORNICATION BY HAVING SEXUAL RELATIONS BEFORE MARRIAGE." [20]

17. And for the same reason He does not permit a married person to debauch himself or herself by COMMITTING ADULTERY. [21] In other words, the rule should be, "Chastity before marriage and fidelity after marriage."

18. Human bodies were designed after the bodies of our Heavenly Father and Heavenly Mother. It is therefore the most abominable of sins to pervert the use of these bodies to any purpose for which they were not designed. God speaks of certain perversions of the functions of the body which are most abominable unto Him. This is what He is referring to when he says, "THOU SHALT NOT COMMIT SODOMY," or, as the Lord told Moses, "Thou shalt not lie with mankind, as with womankind: it is abomination." [22]

19. It is equally abominable for members of the same family or close relatives to engage in sexual relations. Therefore the commandment of God can be summarized as follows: THOU SHALT NOT COMMIT INCEST BY HAVING UNLAWFUL SEXUAL RELATIONS WITH MEMBERS OF YOUR FAMILY OR NEAR RELATIVES. [23]

20. Animal life is of a lower order than the Father's children, and that is why it is an unnatural perversion of the divine order

of things to use animals as sexual partners. As God says, in effect, THOU SHALT NOT COPULATE WITH ANIMALS OF ANY KIND. [24]

21. Entering into a contract or a covenant should be treated as a sacred obligation. A person who honors this divine precept gains the reputation of his word being as good as his bond.

The highest covenant of all is to seal a promise in the name of God. Therefore the Lord has said: "THOU SHALT NOT TAKE THE NAME OF THE LORD THY GOD IN VAIN." [25] God will not be mocked, and he who has made a covenant in the name of the Lord will be required to account for every word of it. This is true for those who make covenants in God's temple. This is also true for those who testify under oath in court, and those who accept high offices and swear to uphold the Constitution.

22. It is very clear from the scriptures that life on this earth is not a free ride. God commands that WORKERS SHALL SEEK TO EARN AN HONEST LIVING AND NOT TO BE SLOTHFUL OR LAZY. [26]

23. By the same token, God requires EMPLOYERS TO PAY AN HONEST WAGE AND NOT OPPRESS THEIR WORKERS. [27]

24. The very nature of life on earth presumes that there will be inequalities and hardships. In God's eyes, the great leveler is the voluntary generosity of those who have accumulated wealth or goods and property beyond their needs. God has a special command for those who have been richly blessed. He says: BE GENEROUS IN HELPING THE POOR. [28] Isaiah said that if a person wonders how to become acceptable to the Lord, here is His answer:

"Is it not to deal thy bread to the hungry, and that thou bring the poor that are cast out to thy house? when thou seest the naked, that thou cover him; and that thou hide not thyself from thine own flesh [who are in desperate need]?" [29]

25. God is especially mindful of those who are in desperate circumstances through no fault of their own and are helpless, unless those who have been blessed with abundance will share with them. He therefore commands that there must be a reaching out to SUCCOR THE WIDOWS AND ORPHANS. [30] Furthermore, it is a sin in the eyes of God to neglect THE HELPLESS AND HANDICAPPED. [31]

26. One of the curses of humanity is the vice of alcoholism or addictive drinks [and in our day, addictive drugs]. All through the scriptures, God looks upon those who let alcohol make them idiotic and irresponsible as committing a great sin against their Maker. He says THOU SHALT NOT BECOME DRUNKEN, [32] and declares that drugs and intoxicants desecrate their bodies which are literally temples of God. [33]

27. In the Beatitudes, the Savior said, "Blessed are the peacemakers: for they shall be called the children of God." [34] He was especially referring to those peacemakers who do not allow themselves to be easily offended. Some people love to make a monumental issue out of the smallest hurt. But these kinds of people have no place in a Zion society. God's people have bigger souls. They follow the admonition of Jesus when He said to shrug off these daily wrongs and inconveniences. His advice was to TURN THE OTHER CHEEK AND GET ON WITH LIFE. [35] This is characteristic of those who want to live in a Zion society.

28. And among Zion people there is another admirable trait. It is a spirit of anxious service. These are people who gladly GO THE SECOND MILE, and when demands are made upon them, they seem willing to give double. [36]

29. The people of a Zion society are neat, carefully groomed, and clean. They do not go about as if they had neither respect nor concern about their appearance or the impression they make on others. It was no casual comment when God said to the wicked Israelites, THOU SHALT WASH YOURSELVES AND MAKE

YOURSELVES CLEAN. He also told them to wash their clothes in preparation for His appearance before them. [37]

30. It is also significant that God expects mankind to BEAUTIFY AND REPLENISH THE EARTH. [38] It is a joy to live in a neighborhood where even the most modest homes are freshly painted and the yards of the homes are filled with flowers and gardens.

31. He also wants His children to talk to Him, explain their problems, and petition for specific needs. To pray to God night and morning—and in between times when necessary—is the standard pattern for the candidates of a Zion society. Jesus said PRAY IN SECRET and USE NOT VAIN REPETITIONS. The Lord wants us to tell Him specifically why we are thankful and what we need. [39]

32. The Lord says to frankly ACKNOWLEDGE AND SEEK TO OVERCOME OUR PERSONAL WEAKNESSES. [40] It seems we never reach a time when we are not plagued with a variety of personal weaknesses.

33. God also knows that in a materialistic world—especially during times of prosperity—the people get caught up in fancy cars, luxurious homes, extravagant clothes, and pet hobbies. These become their treasures and the objects of their time, means and devotion. In a Zion society, everything is beautiful, but the people are busily engaged in BUILDING THEIR TREASURES IN HEAVEN. [41] This comes by obeying God's commandments and continually reaching out to help others.

34. Another quality of a Zion society is the sense of peace and good order. There are no crowds of protesters gathering in the streets or violent crowds making demands on the authorities. Zion-trained people know that God has said THOU SHALT NOT FORM MOBS TO DO EVIL, [42] and He also said, THOU SHALT NOT RIOT. [43] When needs are not met there are peaceful and effective means by which they are remedied and channels of appeal until the situation is resolved.

35. God has prescribed additional commands to preserve honest and efficient government. For example, He has said that PUBLIC SERVANTS SHALL NOT ACCEPT BRIBES. [44]

36. Not only must the judges be above various modes of corruption but they must JUDGE EQUITABLY, TREATING RICH AND POOR ALIKE. [45]

37. Furthermore, the Lord requires all citizens to HONOR AND SUSTAIN LAWFUL GOVERNMENT. [46]

38. God's foreign policy is a simple one. He says man's constant concern should be to ESTABLISH PEACE BETWEEN MEN AND AMONG NATIONS. [47]

39. In a Zion society, there is a constant emphasis on learning. As the Lord said: "And as all have not faith, seek ye diligently and teach one another words of wisdom; yea, SEEK YE OUT OF THE BEST BOOKS words of wisdom; SEEK LEARNING, even by study and also by faith." [48]

40. Some people study a lot, but never organize their information so they can communicate it quickly and clearly to others. It was Peter who said: "BE READY ALWAYS TO GIVE AN ANSWER TO EVERY MAN THAT ASKETH YOU A REASON OF THE HOPE THAT IS IN YOU." [49] This means organizing gospel principles, knowledge of history, concepts of science, etc. so that we can answer questions simply and with satisfying documentation that will inspire confidence in what we teach.

41. The Lord not only admonishes us to organize and store up knowledge, but also STORE UP A REASONABLE AMOUNT OF MATERIAL THINGS so that we can cope with emergencies when they arise. As we read in Proverbs: "Go to the ant, thou sluggard; consider her ways, and be wise: which—having no guide, overseer, or ruler—provideth her meat in the summer, and gathereth her food in the harvest. How long wilt thou sleep, O sluggard? when wilt thou arise out of thy sleep? Yet a little sleep, a

little slumber, a little folding of the hands to sleep: so shall thy poverty come as one that travelleth." [50]

42. Israelites were instructed by the Lord to have a DOUBLE TITHE. The first tithe was to support the work of the Lord. The second tithe was to have liquid resources to travel to the feasts, to make contributions to the poor, or to take care of emergencies. Having a family emergency fund is part of a Zion culture. [51]

43. It is also part of a Zion culture to live within one's means and strive to stay out of debt. Debt is a form of bondage even when it occurs as a result of an emergency. This must be perceived as a necessary evil at best and a temporary state of bondage from which one must escape as soon as possible. Debt must never be accepted as a perpetual way of life. It has destroyed many nations and it has destroyed many families. Here is what the Lord said to those who wanted to enter the Zion society in the early days of the Church: "And again, verily I say unto you, concerning your debts—behold IT IS MY WILL THAT YOU SHALL PAY ALL YOUR DEBTS." [52] Of course, paying debts takes time, and the Lord was well aware of that. But the goal was clear: "Get out of debt as soon as possible."

44. Both in and out of a Zion society, debts tend to make enemies—even among friends—and so does tale-bearing. Irresponsible individuals, afflicted with the psychoneurosis of gossip-mongering, can split a community seven different ways in a single week. It is like a contagion that fouls the environment and thrives on character assassination. A gossip-monger is a sinner in the sight of God. He said: "THOU SHALT NOT GO UP AND DOWN AS A TALEBEARER among thy people." [53] And "Thou shalt not raise a false report: put not thine hand with the wicked to be an unrighteous witness." [54]

45. God contemplates a warm and compassionate relationship among His children here on earth. Over the years, and while traveling through many countries, this writer has come to realize that there is more good will among the general populace

of the earth than one might suppose—especially in times of distress or on occasions of spontaneous rejoicing and celebration. Here is what the prophet Alma observed in a large group of people whom he considered worthy of membership in God's kingdom. To them he said:

"Ye are desirous to come into the fold of God, and to be called his people, and are willing to bear one another's burdens, that they may be light; yea, and are willing to MOURN WITH THOSE THAT MOURN; yea, AND COMFORT THOSE THAT STAND IN NEED OF COMFORT, and to stand as witnesses of God at all times and in all things, and in all places that ye may be in, even until death, that ye may be redeemed of God, and be numbered with those of the first resurrection, that ye may have eternal life." [55] Such is the spirit of Zion.

WHAT WE CAN LEARN FROM THE FAILURE OF THE ZION SOCIETY IN MISSOURI

Because the Lord "knows all things from the beginning," He realized the Zion experiment in Missouri would fail even before it started. Nevertheless, it was a vital part of the preparation of the Saints for the day when the people would be required to live the high-precision specifications of a Zion society in the New Jerusalem which is an important part of our dispensation.

The Lord's principal procedure in teaching His people godly principles is "learning by doing," and an experience in failure is often the most forceful way to provide strict parameters for more perfect obedience to the Lord's commandments in the future. It was so in Missouri.

Nobody can read the Missouri epoch of tragic Church history between 1831 and 1839 without cringing at the suffering and horrible cruelty which the Saints endured. Their dreams of a Zion society crumbled and they found themselves incapable of living the principles which a Zion society requires.

Of course, as a result of their experiences, they gradually learned that their failure was not the fault of the Zion "system," but the fact that they were not seasoned Saints. They were tremendously excited about the prospect of entering a Zion society, but they had not yet conditioned themselves to practice it on the Lord's level of perfection and intensity.

Why did the Lord have them undertake such an assignment when they were merely raw recruits in the army of the Lord? No doubt the answer lies in the fact that their failure provided a vivid historical frame of reference for that future day when the Saints will be required hurriedly to set up God's City of Zion. When that happens, there will be no time for experimental mistakes.

One might well imagine the surge of triumphant joy which illuminated the minds of the Saints who were the first to arrive in Missouri and heard Joseph Smith reveal exactly where God's New Jerusalem would be established in these latter days. [56]

There were about 1,200 members of the Church in the first group to reach Missouri. They had already been told how to set up the law of consecration and how the bishop should distribute the stewardships—or the means of providing a livelihood—for each family. [57]

The Lord's instructions contained a strong emphasis on the need to provide for the poor so that they could have an equal opportunity to become first class citizens in the new Zion society. There were also several revelations about this time, warning certain of the leaders to guard against pride or a superiority complex just because they had been selected for key assignments in the Church or in the new beginning of a Zion society in Missouri.

Having laid down the ground rules, the participants no doubt wondered what the Lord would think of their efforts as they proceeded along the way.

THE FIRST MAJOR ERROR WAS BY THE BISHOP

After Joseph Smith had seen the foundation established and had dedicated the land as the Lord commanded, he returned to Kirtland. Before long, however, he learned that the bishop in charge of the "order" had violated one of the most basic rules of a Zion society.

Apparently Bishop Edward Partridge looked over his flock of new stewards and felt they were not ready to assume complete responsibility for the valuable sections of land he was assigning to them. He therefore reacted to this observation like a businessman, rather than a bishop operating under a revelation in which the Lord had said:

"Every man shall be made accountable unto me, a steward over his OWN property, or that which he has received by consecration, as much as is sufficient for himself and family." [58]

As an experienced businessman, Bishop Edward Partridge decided it would be prudent to LEASE the land to each steward so he could keep an eye on it and make sure the steward was handling his assignment efficiently. But of course this made the bishop the actual owner and the steward merely a sort of share cropper.

When the Lord revealed to Joseph Smith up in Kirtland what was happening, the revelation said:

"I, the Lord God, will send one mighty and strong [apparently the President of the Church], holding the scepter of power in his hand . . . to set in order the house of God, and to arrange by lot the inheritances of the saints whose names are found . . . enrolled in the book of the law of God;

"While that man, who was called of God and appointed, that PUTTETH FORTH HIS HAND TO STEADY THE ARK OF GOD, shall fall by the shaft of death, like as a tree that is smitten by the vivid shaft of lightning." [59]

Three months earlier, when these Saints first arrived in Missouri, the Lord had warned Edward Partridge not to think his judgment was superior to that of his Creator. The Lord had said:

"I have sent you hither, and have selected my servant Edward Partridge, and have appointed unto him his mission in this land. But if he repent not of his sins, which are unbelief and blindness of heart, let him take heed lest he fall. . . .

"And whoso standeth in this mission is appointed to be a judge in Israel, like as it was in ancient days, to divide the lands of the heritage of God unto his children;

"And to judge his people by the testimony of the just . . . according to the laws of the kingdom which are given by the prophets of God . . . Let no man think he is ruler; but let God rule him that judgeth, according to the counsel of his [God's] own will." [60]

ONE ERROR LEADS TO OTHERS

It was the bishop's responsibility to take the "surplus" of the stewards and distribute stewardships to the poor so that in due time "there would be no poor among them."

As time went on, one of the criticisms by the Lord was the fact that there was not an equitable distribution of stewardships TO INCLUDE THE POOR, and the stewards were not contributing their "surplus" to the Lord's "storehouse" so the poor could be accommodated.

Since the bishop had undertaken to use his own wisdom to "steady the Ark of God," he was responsible for these other irregularities that were cropping up in the system. Here was the first and most important lesson to learn from the failure of the Zion experiment in Missouri: STRICTLY ADHERE TO THE PATTERN REVEALED BY THE LORD.

FAILURE TO EARN ZION'S BLESSING REAPS A CURSING

As the Saints began to suffer severe persecution and were completely driven out of Jackson County, they wondered why they were not being blessed and why the Lord did not intervene in their behalf.

In a whole series of revelations, the Lord spelled out their weaknesses and sins. In one revelation to Joseph Smith, the Lord said:

"Verily I say unto you, concerning your brethren who have been afflicted, and persecuted, and cast out from the land of their inheritance—I, the Lord, have suffered the affliction to come upon them, wherewith they have been afflicted, in consequence of their transgressions . . . Therefore, they must be chastened . . . For all those who will not endure chastening, but deny me, cannot be sanctified.

"Behold, I say unto you, there were jarrings, and contentions, and envyings, and strifes, and lustful and covetous desires among them; therefore by these things they polluted their inheritances. They were slow to hearken unto the voice of the Lord their God; therefore, the Lord their God is slow to hearken unto their prayers, to answer them in the day of their trouble. . . .

"Verily I say unto you, notwithstanding their sins, my bowels are filled with compassion towards them. I will not utterly cast them off." [61]

Nevertheless, they were driven out of Missouri. Their enemies violated every law on the books, including the most basic guarantees of the United States Constitution. The crowning offense against human decency and American justice was when Governor Lilburn W. Boggs issued a genocidal extermination order authorizing the mobs-turned-state-militia to drive the people from the state or annihilate them.

Fifteen thousand members of the Church were evacuated from their homes; their barns were burned; their cattle were stolen or slaughtered; their houses were looted and then expropriated or burned; the men were whipped and some of them killed; some of the women were ravished to death; children were scattered and orphaned; the leaders of the Church were imprisoned and sentenced to be shot. At one point, Joseph Smith could not help but cry out, "O God, Where art thou?" [62]

The Lord's reply was comforting, but challenging. Joseph Smith was assured that he and his associates would eventually escape from their murderous captors. However, the Savior compared Joseph's situation with the one He Himself had to endure. This humbled the young prophet and filled him with resolution to bear his cross.

By the close of 1839, the Church had run its gauntlet of the Missouri nightmare. By this time, the Saints had the bitter lessons in Missouri written in their own blood. But in Illinois, they found a refuge and arranged for a new settlement, which in five years became the largest community in the state. They called it Nauvoo—the "Beautiful."

WHO IS READY FOR A ZION SOCIETY TODAY?

It is interesting that one community of Saints built a settlement across the Mississippi from Nauvoo. They called it Montrose. The leaders felt that NOW they could practice the law of consecration and set up stewardships in righteousness. But as soon as Joseph Smith escaped from Missouri and found what they were doing, he halted the whole undertaking and told the people they must never attempt to set up a Zion society until they were commanded to do so by the prophet of the Lord. [63]

Meanwhile, we often hear people say they can hardly wait until they are called up and enlisted in God's Zion society of the latter days. But after reading the tragic experience of the Saints in Missouri from 1831 to 1839, this writer wonders how many of us are spiritually matured and sufficiently refined even to endure—let alone enjoy—the refinements and requirements of a Zion society.

A simple example will illustrate the point. As we have already mentioned, the bishop must follow the parable of the talents or the pounds in making allocations to the various stewards. This means he distributes the "surplus" assets of the Lord's storehouse where he feels they will be "multiplied" to the utmost advantage of the whole society. Supposing your bishop gives his oldest son a choice stewardship and adds to it every year with marvelous facilities and equipment? Or even worse, supposing the son receives the very stewardship you were hoping to get?

Do you have a problem with that?

In a Zion society, we find out whether we really love our neighbor as much as ourselves, or as much as our own children. We learn to turn the other cheek to avoid controversy with the less mature, the less spiritual, the less considerate. This means that when we are offended we forgive and go on about our business without any grudge.

Who is ready for that?

THE NEW JERUSALEM

Although there is a secret hope in each of us that we might someday qualify as a steward in a Zion society, the probability is that not more than one out of ten of us is likely to get a favorable nod from the Lord or His servants until after we undergo a tremendous amount of additional preparation.

To gain some appreciation of the kind of people the Lord will need when it is time to set up a Zion society in the New Jerusalem, let us repeat the description of those who made it in the past. For example, in the days of Christ's Apostles, it says:

"The multitude of them that believed were of one heart and of one soul: neither said any of them that ought of the things which he possessed was his own . . . Neither was there any among them that lacked: for as many as were possessors of lands or houses sold them, and brought the prices of the things that were sold, And laid them down at the apostles' feet: and distribution was made unto every man according as he had need." [64]

In the days of Enoch "the Lord called his people ZION, because they were of one heart and one mind, and dwelt in righteousness; and there was no poor among them." [65]

In the days of Nephi the Fourth, "there was no contention in the land, because of the love of God which did dwell in the hearts of the people. And there were no envyings, nor strifes, nor tumults, nor whoredoms, nor lyings, nor murders, nor any manner of lasciviousness; and surely there could not be a happier people among all the people who had been created by the hand of God." [66]

When the New Jerusalem finally is built, it will be people of this quality who will live there.

* * * *

TOPICS FOR REFLECTION AND DISCUSSION

1. What were the three things that most impressed you in the description of a Zion society by John Adams? What law did he say the people would need to follow?

2. Give a personal experience where you found that you could only enjoy the Zion-type of euphoria a moment at a time. How do you think you would have reacted if you had been present when President Hunter was threatened with an alleged bomb?

3. Why are we especially blessed to have been made a part of our Heavenly Father's kingdom? Where would we be otherwise?

4. Identify ten godly qualities which you feel deserve definite improvement in your own life.

5. Did the Lord know beforehand that the Zion experiment in Missouri would fail? What future advantage will be the failure of the Zion experiment in Missouri to the members of the Church?

6. What specific things did the Lord itemize concerning the Saints in Missouri which demonstrated that they were not yet prepared to undertake the high ideals of the law of consecration?

7. What was the major error made by Bishop Edward Partridge when he distributed the "inheritances" to the people in Missouri? Can you explain why the Lord was so provoked by the attempt of Bishop Partridge to "steady the Ark of God?" What was set forth in the Lord's warning to Bishop Partridge three months earlier?

8. What defect in Bishop Partridge's plan had led to the neglect of the poor? Under his plan, could the people really practice the law of consecration or set up a Zion society?

9. When the people wondered why they were being persecuted and driven out of Jackson County, what were four of the sins of the people specifically identified by the Lord? When Joseph Smith complained, what did the Lord tell him?

10. Would you like to qualify for the opportunity of setting up a Zion society and helping to build the New Jerusalem? On a scale of one to ten, how near do you think you are to qualifying for such a blessing? Are you totally resolved to become fully qualified?

1.   Diary and Autobiography of John Adams, Vol. III, p. 9
2.   Eleanor Knowles, *Howard W. Hunter*, Salt Lake City: Deseret Book Company, 1994, pp. 304-306
3.   For a discussion of this important part of our eternal progression, see W. Cleon Skousen, *The Days of the Living Christ*, vol. 2, pp. 914-915
4.   Luke 10:27
5.   D&C 59:21; Deuteronomy 11:27-28
6.   D&C 19:15
7.   Mark 16:16
8.   D&C 39:23
9.   D&C 14:7

10. Exodus 20:13

11. D&C 42:18

12. Exodus 20:15; Leviticus 19:11

13. Leviticus 19:11; Exodus 20:16; 23:1

14. Exodus 20:17

15. Deuteronomy 11:19

16. 1 Timothy 5:8

17. Exodus 20:12

18. Leviticus 19:18; Matthew 19:19

19. Matthew 7:12

20. 1 Thessalonians 4:2-5

21. Exodus 20:14; 1 Corinthians 6:9

22. Leviticus 18:22; 20:13; Romans 1:27; 1 Corinthians 6:9

23. Leviticus 18:6-16

24. Exodus 22:19

25. Exodus 20:7

26. Proverbs 21:25; Ephesians 4:28; 2 Thessalonians 3:10-12

27. Deuteronomy 24:14-15

28. Deuteronomy 24:14-15; Isaiah 58:7; James 1:27

29. Ibid.

30. Exodus 22:22-24; Deuteronomy 24:19-21; James 1:27

31. Leviticus 19:14

32. Deuteronomy 21:20; Romans 13:13

33. D&C 93:35

34. Matthew 5:9

35. Matthew 5:39

36. Matthew 5:41

37. Isaiah 1:16; Exodus 19:10

38. Genesis 1:28; 2:15

39. Matthew 6:6-7

40. James 5:16; Acts 26:20; Matthew 5:48

41. 3 Nephi 13:19-20

42. Exodus 23:2

43. Romans 13:13; 2 Peter 2:13

44. Deuteronomy 16:19

45. Leviticus 19:15

46. 2 Peter 2:10; Acts 23:5

47. Isaiah 52:7; Romans 2:10; Mark 9:50

48. D&C 88:118
49. 1 Peter 3:15
50. Proverbs 6:6–11
51. Deuteronomy 14:22-29
52. D&C 104:78–79
53. Leviticus 19:16
54. Exodus 23:1
55. Mosiah 18:8–9
56. D&C 57:2-3
57. D&C Section 42
58. D&C 42:32
59. D&C 85:7–8
60. D&C 58:14–20
61. D&C 101:1–9
62. D&C 121:1
63. *History of the Church*, vol. 4, p. 93
64. Acts 4:32–35
65. Moses 7:18
66. 4 Nephi 1:15–16

LOOKING FORWARD

After I received my patriarchal blessing at age fourteen, the patriach told me that he didn't share everything with me. That bothered me because I wanted to know! So I asked him to tell me what he left out, but he said "no" because he didn't think it would be prudent.

As I think back on that wise patriarch, I shudder at the thought of what it would have done to my young personality had it been revealed to me at that age the terribly difficult challenges and responsibilities I would and have had throughout my life. It would have scared the daylights out of me!

GOD COMMANDS NEPHI NOT TO REVEAL TOO MUCH

One of God's prophets, Nephi, when he was about 16, was allowed to see the entire history of mankind. As Nephi recorded what he was seeing, he got right up to sometime in our day when an angelic being commanded him to stop writing. He was told he would continue to see how it all turned out, but it would be another prophet, named John the Revelator, who would have the privilege of recording it.

Years later, having left Jerusalem with his family and migrated by ship to the Western Hemisphere, Nephi began reading Isaiah who had lived 100 years earlier. To his astonishment, Nephi found that Isaiah saw what Nephi had seen. So Nephi decided to do an interesting thing. He placed in the Book of Mormon various chapters of Isaiah and then commented on them. Nephi knew exactly how it was going to turn out, and here was someone who already had written it down, so he added that to the record.

Toward the end of recording First Nephi, he had already written the good news about the gospel being restored, Israel beginning to be gathered, and then suddenly Nephi says, "And now, I Nephi make an end for I durst not speak further as yet." [1]

I think he's yearning to tell us some more good news.

Later, when Nephi was an old man, he recorded fourteen more chapters of Isaiah. Beginning in about 2 Nephi 25, he said he would tell us again what Isaiah saw—Nephi points out that he saw the same thing (2 Nephi 26:7). But then in 2 Nephi 32:7, just as he gets to our present day, he says, "And now, I Nephi cannot say more; the Spirit stoppeth mine utterance."

Had the Spirit allowed Nephi to continue recording, what would he have written? If he had written, "everything will come out all right," what would that do to the missionary program? What would that do to your anxiety?

Or if Nephi had written, "No matter what you do, the Church will ultimately fail," what would that do to your ambition?

This is why the Spirit of the Lord commanded Nephi not to write it. So, we just don't know how things will end up for America. But it is the opinion of this author that because of the way Nephi handled this, there is great news ahead of us and we are going to be all right.

GOD MAKES A PROMISE

Our Heavenly Father assures us in D&C 97:25 that we have an insurance policy no matter what happens, if we stay close to the Lord. And the righteous Gentiles—good Christians who love Christ—also have an insurance policy. And those who are peacemakers and don't want to be drafted into the second dictatorship, they have a promise. [2]

I am so grateful to know the gospel is back on the earth. I am thankful that God has revealed so much to give us courage for the difficult days that lie ahead, knowing that if we are in our places, doing what we should be doing, all will be well—

All will be well!

---

1. 1 Nephi 22:29
2. D&C 45:66-71; D&C 115:6?

APPENDIX

A DREAM

BY CHARLES D. EVANS, PATRIARCH

(Printed in THE CONTRIBUTOR, Vol. 15, No. 10

August, 1894, pp. 638-641)

While I lay pondering, in deep solitude, on the events of the present my mind was drawn into a reverie such as I had never felt before. A strong solicitude for my imperiled country utterly excluded every other thought and raised my feelings to a point of intensity I did not think it possible to endure. While in this solemn, profound and painful reverie of mind, to my infinite surprise, a light appeared in my room, which seemed to be soft and silvery as that diffused from a northern star. At the moment of its appearance the acute feeling I had experienced instantly yielded to one of calm tranquility.

Although it may have been at the hour of midnight, and the side of the globe whereon I was situated was excluded from the sunlight, yet all was light and bright and warm as an Italian landscape at noon; but the heat was softer or more subdued. As I gazed upward, I saw descending through my bedroom roof, with a gently gliding movement, a personage clothed in white apparel, whose countenance was smoothly serene, his features regular, and the flashes of his eye seemed to shoot forth scintillations, to use an earthly comparison, strongly resembling those reflected from a diamond under an intensely illuminated electric light, which dazzled but did not bewilder. Those large, deep, inscrutable eyes were presently fixed upon mine, when instantly placing his hands upon my forehead his touch produced an indescribable serenity and calmness, a calmness not born of earth, but at once peaceful, delightful and heavenly. My whole being was imbued with a joy unspeakable. All feelings of sorrow instantly vanished. Those lines and shadows which care and sorrow impress upon us were dispelled as a deep fog before a blazing sun. In the eyes of my heavenly visitor, for such he appeared to me, there was a sort of lofty pity and tenderness infinitely stronger than any such feeling I ever saw manifested in ordinary mortals. His very calm appeared like a vast ocean stillness, at once overpowering to every agitated emotion.

By some intuition, or instinct, I felt he had something to communicate to soothe my sorrows and allay my apprehensions. Whereon, addressing me, he said:

"Son, I perceive thou hast grave anxieties over the perilous state of thy country, that thy soul has felt deep sorrow for its future. I have therefore come to thy relief and to tell thee of the causes that have led to this peril. Hear me attentively. Seventy-one years ago [about 1823], after an awful apostasy of centuries, in which all nations were shrouded in spiritual darkness, when the angels had withdrawn themselves, the voice of prophets hushed, and the light of Urim and Thummim shone not, and the vision of the seers was closed, while heaven itself shed not a ray of gladness to lighten a dark world, when Babel ruled and Satan laughed, and church and priesthood had taken their upward flight, and the voice of nations, possessing the books of the Jewish prophets, had ruled against vision and against Urim, against the further visits of angels, and against the doctrine of a church of apostles and prophets, thou knowest that then appeared a mighty angel with the solemn announcement of the hour of judgment, the burden of whose instructions pointed to dire calamities upon the present generation. This, therefore, is the cause of what thou seest and the end of the wicked hasteneth."

My vision now became extended in a marvelous manner, and the import of the past labors of the Elders was made plain to me. I saw multitudes fleeing to the place of safety in our mountain heights. The church was established in the wilderness. Simultaneously the nation had reached an unparalleled prosperity, wealth abounded, new territory was acquired, commerce extended, finance strengthened, confidence was maintained, and peoples abroad pointed to her as the model nation, the ideal of the past realized and perfected, the embodiment of the liberty sung by poets, and sought for by sages.

"But," continued the messenger, "Thou beholdest a change. Confidence is lost. Wealth is arrayed against labor, labor against wealth, yet the land abounds with plenty for food and raiment, and silver and gold are in abundance. Thou seest also that letters written by a Jew have wrought great confusion in the finances of the nation which, together with the policy of many wealthy ones, has produced distress and do presage further sorrow."

Factions now sprang up as if by magic: capital had entrenched itself against labor throughout the land; labor was organized against capital. The voice of the wise sought to tranquilize these two powerful factors in vain. Excited multitudes ran wildly about; strikes increased; lawlessness sought the place of regular government. At this juncture I saw a banner floating in air whereon was written the words BANKRUPTCY, FAMINE, FLOODS, FIRE, CYCLONES, BLOOD, PLAGUE. Mad with rage men and women rushed upon each other. Blood flowed down the streets of cities like water. The demon of bloody hate had enthroned itself on the citadel of reason; the thirst for blood was intenser than that of the parched tongue for water. Thousands of bodies lay entombed in the streets. Men and women fell dead from the terror inspired by fear. Rest was but the precursor of the bloody work of the morrow. All around lay the mournfulness of a past in ruins. Monuments erected to perpetuate the names of the noble and brave were ruthlessly destroyed by combustibles. A voice now sounded aloud these words, "Yet once again I shake not the earth only, but also heaven. And this word yet once again signifies the removing of things that are shaken, as of things that are made; that those things that cannot be shaken may remain."

Earthquakes rent the earth in vast chasms, which engulfed multitudes; terrible groanings and wailings filled the air; the shrieks of the suffering were indescribably awful. Water wildly rushed in from the tumultuous ocean whose very roaring under the mad rage of the fierce cyclone, was unendurable to the ear. Cities were swept away in an instant, missiles were hurled through the atmosphere at a terrible velocity and people were carried upward only to descend an unrecognized mass. Islands appeared where ocean waves once tossed the gigantic steamer. In other parts voluminous flames, emanating from vast fires, rolled with fearful velocity destroying life and property in their destructive course. The seal of the dread menace of despair was stamped on every human visage; men fell exhausted, appalled and trembling. Every element of agitated nature seemed a demon of wrathful fury. Dense clouds, blacker than midnight darkness, whose thunders reverberated with into-nations which shook the earth, obscured the sunlight. Darkness reigned, unrivaled and supreme.

Again the light shone, revealing an atmosphere tinged with a leaden hue, which was the precursor of an unparalleled plague whose first symptoms were recognized by a purple spot which appeared on the cheek, or on the back of the hand, and which invariably enlarged until it spread over the entire surface of the body, producing certain death. Mothers, on sight of it, cast away their children as if they were poisonous reptiles. This plague, in grown persons, rotted the eyes in their sockets and consumed the tongue as would a powerful acid or an intense heat. Wicked men, suffering under its writhing agonies, cursed God and died, as they stood on their feet, and the birds of prey feasted on their carcasses.

I saw in my dream the messenger again appear with a vial in his right hand, who addressed me saying: "Thou knowest somewhat of the chemistry taught in the schools of human learning; behold now a chemistry sufficiently powerful to change the waters of the sea."

He then poured out his vial upon the sea and it became putrid as the blood of a dead man, and every living soul therein died. Other plagues followed I forbear to record.

A foreign power had inroaded [1] the nation which, from every human indication, it appeared would seize the government and supplant it with monarchy. I stood trembling at the aspect, when, lo, a power arose in the west which declared itself in favor of the Constitution in its original form; to this suddenly rising power every lover of constitutional rights and liberties throughout the nation gave hearty support. The struggle was fiercely contested, but the stars and stripes floated in the breeze, and, bidding defiance to all opposition, waved proudly over the land. Among the many banners I saw, was one inscribed thus: "The government based on the Constitution, now and forever. On another, "Liberty of Conscience, social, religious, and political."

The light of the gospel which had but dimly shone because of abomination, now burst forth with a lustre that filled the earth. Cities appeared in every direction, one of which, in the centre of the continent, was an embodiment of architectural science after the pattern of eternal perfections, whose towers glittered with a radiance emanating from the sparkling of emeralds, rubies, diamonds and other precious stones set in a canopy of gold and so elaborately and skillfully arranged as to shed forth a brilliance which dazzled and enchanted the eye, excited admiration and developed a taste for the beautiful, beyond anything man had ever conceived.

Fountains of crystal water shot upward their transparent jets which in the brilliant sunshine, formed ten thousand rainbow tints at once delightful to the eye. Gardens, the perfections of whose arrangement confound all our present attempts at genius, were bedecked with flowers of varied hue to develop and refine the taste, and strengthen a love for these nature's chastest adornments.

Schools and universities were erected, to which all had access; in the latter Urims were placed, for the study of the past, present and future, and for obtaining a knowledge of the heavenly bodies, and of the constructions of worlds and universes. The inherent properties of matter, its arrangements, laws, mutual relations were revealed and taught and made plain as the primer lesson of a child. The conflicting theories of the geologists regarding the formation and age of the earth were settled forever. All learning was based on eternal certainty. Angels brought forth the treasures of knowledge which had lain hid in the womb of the dumb and distant past.

The appliances for making learning easy surpass all conjecture. Chemistry was rendered extremely simple, by the power which the Urims conferred on man of looking into and through the elements of every kind; a stone furnished no more obstruction to human vision than the air itself. Not only were the elements and all their changes and transformations plainly understood, but the construction, operations, and laws of mind were thus rendered equally plain as those which governed the coarser elements.

While looking through the Urim and Thummim, I was amazed at the transformation which even now is to me marvelous beyond description, clearly showing the manner in which particles composing the inorganic kingdom of nature are conducted upward to become a part of organic forms; another astounding revelation was a view clearly shown me of the entire circulation of blood both in man and animals. After seeing these things and gazing once more upon the beautiful city, the following passage of scripture sounded in my ears: "Out of Zion, the perfection of beauty, God shineth."

On this I awoke to find all a dream.

—CHARLES D. EVANS

---

1. Inroaded, to make in-roads, to penetrate or invade but not overwhelm

ANOTHER VISION

ATTRIBUTED TO CHARLES D. EVANS

Charles D. Evans, on December 15, 1882, saw in mighty vision: the "enslaving of one portion of the children of freedom who differed from them in religious belief and practice." Then he saw "the bands that held society together during the reign of the Republic, were snapped asunder . . . Political strife was everywhere . . . Blood was written on every banner."

The Angel said: "Look again." I looked and beheld that many who were angry with the rulers of the Republic, for their subversion of the Constitutional Law, and their wholesale plunder of the Public moneys, arose and proclaimed themselves the friends of the Constitution in its original form . . . A voice was now suddenly heard declaring these words: "In the distant mountain tops are to be found the true lovers of freedom and equal rights . . . Go there" . . . when suddenly appeared on Ensign Peak near Salt Lake City, a beautiful flag standing for Human Liberty throughout the world . . . Tyrants were hurled down . . . one unbroken nation whose BANNER waved for all the world. (Ensign of Nations, p. 11)

INDEX

Symbols

144,000
Not subject to death, 56–57
Orson Pratt describes sealings of, 55
Qualities of, 54
Sealing of, 54, 57
Task to warn and seal up, 57

A

ADAM-ONDI-AHMAN
Conference at, 33
Daniel comments on conference at, 33
Lucifer loses power, 33

ADAMS, JOHN
Comments on Zion Society, 125
Constitution only for moral, religious people, 79

ADAMS, SAMUEL
Liberty not suited to a corrupt people, 79

ALBANY
Will be destroyed if they reject God, 16

ALCOHOL, 134

AMERICA
God's Law and Zion a part of, 98
How will it be cleansed?, 11
Luke, vision of A. sealed off, 25
Nine events precede divine destiny, 1–2
Sealing off the western hemisphere, 23, 25
To become "Kingdom of God," 39
U.S. flag to endure, 40

ANGLO-SAXONS, 67, 68, 71, 72

APOSTATES
Cleansed from the Church, 13

ARMAGEDDON
Battle of, 48

ARTICLE OF FAITH
Wentworth letter, 45

ATHEISM
Adolf Hitler's contributions, 7
Alfred C. Kinsey contributions, 8
Benito Mussolini's contributions, 7
Karl Marx's contributions, 7
Sigmund Freud's contributions, 7

B

BALTIMORE
Dead piled high, John Taylor vision, 15

BEATITUDES
Turn the other cheek, 134

BOSTON
Will be destroyed if they reject God, 16

C

CHAOS
Covers the earth, 52

CHRIST
Warning to wicked in America, 5
Wounds in Christ's hands and feet?, 50

CHURCH
Cleansed of apostates and backsliders, 13